HEAR us ROAR
TIGER EDITION

Copyright © KMD Books
First published in Australia in 2025
by KMD Books
Waikiki, WA 6169

All rights reserved. No part of this book may be used or reproduced by any means, graphic, electronic, or mechanical, including photocopying, recording, taping or by any information storage retrieval system without the written permission of the copyright owner except in the case of brief quotations embodied in critical articles and reviews.

Because of the dynamic nature of the Internet, any web addresses or links contained in this book may have changed since publication and may no longer be vaild. The views expressed in this work are solely those of the author and do not necessarily reflect the views of the publisher and the publisher hereby disclaims any responsibility for them.

A catalogue record for this work is available from the National Library of Australia

National Library of Australia Catalogue-in-Publication data:
Hear Us Roar: Tiger Edition/KMD Books

CONTENTS

Adrea L Peters
Twenty More Years 1

Bek Paroz
Powerfully On Purpose 8

Cathy Domoney
The Power to Choose 16

Christopher Kai
The Sales Spell 24

Deborah Dickinson
Brave Enough to Begin Again 38

Emma Weaver
Building Mental Wealth 48

Kabinga Mazaba
Endurance Beyond the Stripes of Challenges 61

Karen Weaver
Finding Purpose 72

Laura Muirhead
A Recipe for Success.. 79

Louise Lally
The Power of Borrowed Belief 87

Maraika Mason
Early Life Changes... 93

Marianne Rose
A Letter to my Niece 100

Melissa Homewood
Dis-Ease 107

Michael Tellis
A Journey to Find Deep Purpose 116

Mike Mackay
Penning Existence 126

Nicole Whitty
The Dream.. 136

Robyn Verrall
Fuelled By Passion, Driven by Purpose........................... 146

Saoirse Connolly
The Voice of My Womb 155

Scharrell Jackson
The Strength Within.. 165

Sheleila D'Paiva
Empowering Women, One Step at a Time... 174

Val Quinn
Barcelona Full Ironman 182

Vikki Speller
You Are The Purpose 191

ADREA L PETERS
TWENTY MORE YEARS

I waited. Alone. In a sterile, cold waiting area. The cathedral ceiling loomed above me like silent archbishops, their gaze testing my ability to believe. At twenty-eight years old, my father, a man I was only beginning to truly know, was undergoing a kidney transplant. His donor: my step-mom, Ann – the woman I love with every fibre of my being. Two parents. One me. And all I could think about was the terrifying possibility of losing one of them – or both. The thought of never knowing my father as an adult consumed me; so much left unsaid, so many questions to ask, so much of him to understand.

When Dr Osario finally appeared in the waiting room with the news, I was a ball of raw emotion. The words 'everything went well' felt like a rebirth. I embraced him with an intensity that startled me. Never in my life had I experienced such gratitude, such relief. And never had I felt the weight of stress lift so suddenly, as though it had never existed.

For months, my heart and mind had been ensnared in my father's health, wrapped in the urgency of him surviving the surgery. For days, the three of us had been united in a singular purpose; to make it through. But now, the focus shifted to healing. Before this moment, I had been grieving the loss of a future I feared we might never share. It's a strange gift, to prepare for someone's death without it happening. In that space, appreciation floods the soul. The energy to communicate with raw honesty, to embrace vulnerability, becomes essential.

I wanted to ask my dad everything that haunted me from my youth: *Why did you leave? Why the divorces? What were your reasons, your views, your truths?*

In so many ways, Craig Peters and I were replicas – physically, emotionally, in our preferences and pet peeves, our humour and flaws. We were mirrors. And that created tension between us – until it didn't. Until his life hung in the balance and we had to face the fear of him slipping away again.

He left when I was two, and for years, I didn't blame him. It made sense to me. My mother had a way of pushing everyone away. She had a knack for making others uncomfortable, and that sometimes included me. I came to understand that her distance was both a defence and a freedom. It was only when I turned eighteen that I could truly stand on my own and break free of her hold. Despite decades of effort, I never felt I fully convinced her of my unconditional love for her.

But my father, the man who left, grew into a man I admired with all my heart; a man who wielded humour and clarity to share his imperfections. He became my best friend, the one person who truly saw and understood me. And now, as his kidney transplant loomed, I feared we might never have the chance to truly connect on a deeper level, as adults.

The passion and purpose that surged within me at twenty-eight propelled me to a new understanding of life. These deep, challenging moments were not merely obstacles but opportunities – legacy-defining opportunities. I had to quickly and decisively face everything with open eyes. Suddenly, I had to live with intention and purpose. When we confront the fragility of life – our own or someone else's – our mortality flashes before us, a reminder of how precious every moment is. And from that confrontation comes a fire, a flame that burns away the confusion, the hesitation and the excuses, leaving only the truth of who we are and what we're here for.

When we think we've reached the end of our road, the end of ourselves, we are often called to rise. We are invited to evolve into something more than we were before, something better. We brace ourselves for the fall, believing we won't survive it – until we do. And then, from that moment forward, we are changed forever.

As I sat there, thinking of my dad, wondering if we would ever have the chance to speak, to laugh, to love each other again, I questioned how I could possibly go on without him. And then came the miracle. The gift of another chance; to begin again with him by my side. It changed me. It evolved me. And I promised myself then, I would live boldly, fully and as joyfully as I could – for the rest of my days.

The possibility of death gave me passion, it gave me purpose. It helped me live from my truest place; vulnerable, strong, compassionate and open. All the rage I'd carried for past wrongs dissipated. What was the point of dwelling on what couldn't be changed when there was so much to live for, so much in front of me?

The clarity that came with my father's survival was profound, a revelation I struggled to fully comprehend. I threw myself into life with a ferocity I hadn't known before. I said *yes* to everything. And it was exactly what I needed.

I'd always told myself a story about people who had stable, grounded childhoods – those with a clear, supportive foundation – and how I hadn't had that. My childhood had been colourful but unstable. Yet, at twenty-eight, I found myself standing on solid ground, surrounded by the love and support of my father and stepmother. For the first time, I had a foundation, something to lean on, something that would keep me grounded while I explored life.

I revelled in that security. I cherished it. It infused me with energy, with a confidence I'd never known before. I travelled. I ran races. I mountain-biked and snowboarded as though every day was my last. I wrote screenplays. I went to nutrition school. I earned a graduate degree in novel writing. I studied physics and souls and religions. I broke old patterns. I loved and was loved. I began to understand who I was in ways I never had before. I discovered how I operate in the world, how I feel and think, befriend and communicate. How I hurt, heal, let go and commit fully. And I shared every bit of it with my dad and Ann. It was, and remains, a miracle.

Passion and purpose for life came to me when I was faced with the near loss of the man who knew me better than anyone else; my dad. And I was given twenty more years with him.

Twenty. More. Years.

If that's not a miracle, I don't know what is.

Not long after the surgery, I visited my parents at their remote property in Idaho, nestled in the Sawtooth Mountains. On frigid mornings, my dad would make coffee and I would crawl into their tent, snuggle under the covers, and we'd sip our coffee together – talking about bears, of all things. One morning, he was writing in his journal with serious focus.

'What are you writing?' I asked.

'All the things I think I can get done in the next ten years,' he replied.

I knew what he meant; ten years was how long the kidney would likely last. I didn't want to say it. The thought of an expiry date on my dad was unbearable.

'I'm on a bit of a clock now,' he said, with that wry smile.

Ann and I exchanged a teary glance.

'What's on it?' I finally asked.

'Well ...' he said, listing off a few things I've long since forgotten.

That list never came up again. But looking back now, I understand more. It was his way of facing the future, of setting intentions, of giving himself something to strive for. It was his way to process, to heal, to live again. And I wish I'd understood then, because that list, those goals probably haunted him as much as they drove him to exceed them. We learn, when we're ready, that passion and purpose are what keep us alive,

HEAR US ROAR: TIGER EDITION

what make life meaningful, what help us rise above the shadows to live and love fully.

ABOUT ADREA

Adrea Peters is a storyteller, weaving tales that dive deep into love, logic, wellbeing and human potential. Her mission? To remind you that *you* are the hero of your life's story. A valedictorian with a journalism degree from the University of Colorado at Boulder, she later earned master's in popular fiction writing from Seton Hill University.

In March 2025, she was given the top spot for the Top 20 Most Inspiring Women to Watch in 2025. Her impressive body of work spans novels, screenplays and articles. The *Becoming Truitt Skye* trilogy marked her fiction debut in 2020. Bestselling *Quantum Thinking* offers powerful affirmations to unlock your potential.

Adrea and publishing powerhouse Karen Weaver co-host the groundbreaking *A?K TV* and together they crafted *Quantum Love* in 2021. The two's long-awaited release of *The Power of the Pause* will be released in 2025.

Adrea's collaborative spirit also shines through transformative works like *When I Go Outside, I Go Inside* with Teffanie Thompson and *Quantum Wealth* with Amber Lilyestrom. Notably, *Quantum Thinking* and *When I Go Outside, I Go Inside* were in the 2021 Academy Award gift bags.

A mentor for over three decades, Adrea fuels the growth of writers

HEAR US ROAR: TIGER EDITION

with her workshops and her award-winning book, *The Science of Story*. Recognised as one of *Brainz* magazine's Top 500 Entrepreneurs, she was an honoured finalist at the Women Changing the World Global Awards in April 2025.

Adrea loves to connect. Please stop by adreapeters.com and @adreapeters2025 and send her a message!

BEK PAROZ
POWERFULLY ON PURPOSE

The art of motivating yourself is arduous to learn. Once practised, channelling passion, purpose, drive and focus can be easy when you have the support, time, space … and all things that align to make the dream work.

But when times are tough, when the team isn't even present, or life is overwhelming in its intensity, how then can you remain powerfully on purpose?

There is a rise in recognition, accompanying the growing realisation in the mental health space surrounding the impact of undiagnosed trauma, PTSD, ADHD and spectrum disorders. The resulting disruption to the narrative, that 'focus' looks male, professional and quiet, is finally being challenged.

No longer is the look of a studious worker, the only model of purpose. And the ecstatic nature of passion is being explored and has become less sexualising in nature. Though it still has its links to hysteria, in women particularly, and that narrative is slow to change.

I have been told numerous times to be 'less'. Told by so many male bosses that if I were less intense, less passionate, I would be more balanced. *More like them.*

Why is that acceptable? Why is that the narrative we subscribe to when our own natures rebel against it? Why … when words like passion and vision inspire big feelings and resultant actions?

Humans come with built-in emotional connections to their world, their life and their goals. It seems perfectly natural and acceptable in some spaces, but not others. Who determined that filter and how do we challenge the idea that passion is misplaced when we are given that feedback?

'The reasonable man adapts himself to the world; the unreasonable one persists in trying to adapt the world to himself. Therefore, all progress depends on the unreasonable man.' – George Bernard Shaw

It offers the idea that passion, motivation, a different viewpoint, an outside-the-box kind of thinker, is perhaps what is needed in times of change, for leadership and, ultimately, for progress.

After all, individually, socially, professionally and globally, we are wired for progress. Efficient, cheaper, faster, quicker, smarter, lighter, prettier ... whatever your measure, someone is trying to progress that space beyond where it currently is.

The people who push that type of progress question what is, they ask *'why not?'* and challenge the way things have always been done. They do not usually think that a flat line reflects progress or improvement.

So, why then, when words such as passion, or purpose are used with conviction, does the response come with such baggage, as to cause some men to lecture and discuss 'balance'; and some women to immediately decide which outfit works for world-conquering?

How are you emotionally responding to these concepts? How many times have you felt moved passionately to act, driven with purpose toward a goal, only to be told to calm down, or take your time, or even that you are *just too much?* If you're an older woman, you may hear words such as hysterical, manic and hyperactive. If you are a younger woman, you've probably been told that you need to listen to advice from your elders or that your enthusiasm will wear off eventually.

Either way, your excitement, focus and drive will have been brought into question the minute you display elevated emotions. Because of course, that's all passion is, right? Just a bit over-excited, with too much enthusiasm.

Who set the benchmark for 'too much' anyway?

When did enthusiasm become a bad thing or require policing? And when did it become a weaponised word to diminish another's joy in a project, a goal or an outcome they want to achieve?

Maybe you have never had your passion used against you, and if so, I congratulate you on that. Most women will have had an interaction somewhere in their life that has taught them to reduce their impact, to turn down their light, to perhaps remember that others might respond badly to their passion.

How sad that passion is so terrifying. Challenging anything as structured as process and procedure is inherently difficult, resistance to change is understandable. When accompanied by what is perceived as an emotional state, and not a practical one, such as passion versus motivation, resistance to the change can become an emotional response.

Passion can be intimidating. It is intense and can manifest in a myriad of ways.

Motivation and drive are similar words invoking action and focus, but lack the emotional charge of the word *passion*.

Purpose collated into a mission statement and corporate values is an acceptable form and use of the word. Being motivated by those values is honoured professionally.

Being passionate about those values is seen as a boundary cross-over into the personal arena when used. It invokes the idea of a zealot, or someone who is 'over-reactive'.

It's easy to get swept up in the view of others – the social, professional and political ramifications of being identified with 'passion' – and deny part of our nature in order to fit in.

A balance is needed, so as not to overwhelm team members who may not feel such passionate purpose about their role; whether it be the family team, sporting group, or in a professional workplace. Not everyone needs to be operating at that level, not at the same time, and it doesn't necessarily manifest in the same way every time passion is used with purpose. Intense focus, excitable brainstorming, planned communication, these are all forms of passion demonstrated.

However your passion manifests, and the resultant challenge you might face to maintain or sustain the energy of your purpose, what follows is a brief discussion on concepts that can be useful to consider, as you move forward towards your goals, powerfully, passionately and purposefully.

These are common factors many of us can focus on to maintain our sense of connection to self. Hopefully, these ideas will support you through those moments when passion is absent, or dangerous, or even just when you need reminding of your purpose.

SCHEDULE

Downtime is the first thing that tends to be neglected when passion is alight. While the fulfilment of a passionate goal is good for us, so is a break – some relief from that adrenalin high of achievement and a deliberate focus on relaxation. Scheduling that downtime is an important first step, but committing to it and not letting it become a casualty of passion is just as critical for long term mental health wellness.

Feedback and time to evaluate clearly, both positive and negative commentary, is important for your own growth. Being able to filter it through the view of others, in understanding how your passion might impact them, is valuable in many ways. Taking to heart feedback that is offered, more to manage your emotional state, is less useful. Deciding for yourself which feedback is valid can take time and space. And isn't supported in a heightened passionate state sometimes, especially if the feedback has also been delivered passionately.

Disagreement can be labelled as passionate, but care is needed during passionate disagreement to de-escalate. Not all passion is used fairly or equally. Being clear on how feedback is delivered within your team is critical to being respectful, allowing good communication to be valued and working towards making space for passion to be a safe value.

Managing the negative use of passion is a skill to ensure you have, as you work towards making others comfortable in this space. After all, your own journey towards the same things is your shared and valuable experience. Learning to share passion amongst team members is a valuable skill when harnessed positively.

Allowing for 'blips' to rock the purpose, as well as your conviction, is practical. One of the main reasons that 'they' often use as advice against a passionate stance, is that the opposite can be perceived as a significant mood swing. The emotional state considered the opposite of passion is cold or apathetic – emotional words. Undesirable states, yes, but also a comment on the feeling, rather than the energy.

When interruptions to the plan ruffle passion, the opposite state can be emotional, but how many of us who identify with passion also know that it is a state that can be applied to an issue. Being perceived as having a state of quiet reflection on the outer, does not necessarily reflect the inner passionate nature of the thoughts needed in a time and space to match your state, as part of your process.

Those who have never used the idea of passion with process in this way may struggle to understand the comfort of this territory, and perhaps, some have never looked at passion as an inner state that doesn't have to be reflected in big actions and outcomes.

Recognising the ways in which you use passion as an expression of yourself, both externally and internally, can provide insight into managing the lower moments when passion may ebb.

ETHICS

Another myth about passion is that it can cause impetuous behaviour or rapid decision-making that may not be a good choice 'if calmer heads prevail'. While this may be true in some instances, recognising those moments and applying the same decision-making processes every time can support your purpose, instead of hindering your progress. Passion doesn't replace systems or remove the need for the mundane in business and life, so be prepared for times when passion is simply absent. Don't see it as a failure of your values if you can't always be 'on'. See it as a chance to learn to value that downtime, as much as you may value the intensity that passion can bring to a situation. Remembering that you add value in so many other ways is important, as you fulfil your purpose of being true to all your states.

Ethical challenges don't have to kill passion. While your core values may be challenged, a true leader is able to embrace change as a part of feedback and self-improvement. Setting an example in this space allows others to also feel safer about change. When teams know they have an ethical foundation that doesn't change, based on passion alone, they will feel safe about the consistency that can be held in the same space as passion. For those who embrace consistency as a value, this is important to the cohesion of your team long-term, which in turn supports the realisation of your purpose.

CONSISTENCY

Putting your purpose as a priority above your personal triggers and potential negative reactions is an important skill to practise. Powerful people know themselves and show up for their purpose consistently. This value is part of what can keep you connected to passion, even when life is serving up lemons. It reminds you to focus on the outcome, at times, when the details may be overwhelming. When the personal is a distraction from your purpose, it's time to have other areas to channel that passion into. Moving away from the situation, when you are unable to be consistent, is just as valuable as knowing when to come back refreshed.

Consistent focus on areas of mental wellbeing, physical health and life outside of your main passion can provide a balance to the intensity that a passionate life can bring. Keeping momentum by practising consistency, allows for times when passion is hard to maintain. When your passion is exhausting, perhaps it is time to let regular habits move you forward. Recognising those times when it seems harder than usual to focus on your purpose, and having strategies in place that are familiar and effective, can make the difference between remaining powerfully on purpose and getting lost in the personal or negative.

Your passion is something to honor and value. Embracing this part of your nature can reduce fear of being judged and expand possibilities for your dreams, goals, outcomes. Whether it is a personal best, a project, a platform or a professional story that you are writing as the author of your life, allow to power of passion to infuse you.

Remember when you roar, the intent is to be heard.

Make it count.

Make it yours.

Make it passionate.

Make it possible.

ABOUT BEK

Bek is a woman who knows how to roar. Not only has she worked in the senior management arena of the construction industry for over twenty years in Australia, she is an internationally recognised author, an award-winning speaker and a survivor of corporate PTSD, childhood abuse, and is living proof that her long-term disability and neurodiversity are a label like any other.

Bek's passion for living a full live shows up in her purpose: the desire to embrace living fully, supporting others to feel safe, empowered and educated to attempt the same. She embodies the living power of applying passion and purpose in overcoming life and its lemons. Continuing to revive and recreate herself as she moves towards her next bucket list of achievements, Bek continues to believe passion is critical in changing the world and encouraging more women to roar loudly.

CATHY DOMONEY
THE POWER TO CHOOSE

Blindfolded, I stepped into the circle.

I was five years old – small, sensitive and surrounded by my much older siblings and parents. To them, it was just a game. To me, it felt like a test. One I hadn't prepared for. One I wasn't sure I could win.

The rules were simple: I had to feel each family member's face and guess who they were. My little hands, shaky and unsure, moved from cheek to chin to hair. Then, I felt them – my mother's glasses. I lit up. 'Mummy!' I shouted.

Everyone laughed.

The blindfold was removed, and there, in front of me, stood my brother.

The sting of shame rushed through me. I cried. And instead of comfort, I was disciplined.

In that moment, a belief was born: *Don't trust anyone. People will trick you. You are not safe. No one has your back.*

I didn't know it then, but that message – reinforced in quiet, subtle, persistent ways – would shape how I showed up in the world … for decades. That moment was the beginning of many things:

- A fear of getting it wrong.
- A habit of masking my emotions.
- The quiet burying of my true voice.

I grew up in a narcissistic household. I was the youngest by more than a decade, born into a family that already had a rhythm I never quite belonged to. It didn't take long to realise that being small, quiet, and invisible was the safest path. I learned not to rock the boat. Not to speak up. Not to need anything.

Experts would later call what I experienced 'little t' trauma – the kind of wounds that don't leave visible scars but imprint deeply. A slow erosion of self-worth. The feeling of being dismissed, misinterpreted or emotionally abandoned in thousands of tiny ways.

These moments compounded over time, chipping away at my confidence and identity. I became hyper-aware of everyone's moods. I performed peacekeeping before I could even spell the word. I learned to be what others needed – never what I needed.

And yet, in hindsight, I can see it all as preparation. Not punishment. A divine apprenticeship for the work I was destined to do.

In my late teens, I experienced what the world would label 'big T' trauma. A distressing event that left me raw and reeling. I shut down for six months. Not a word. Not a tear. I turned inward and disappeared. To speak about it would have unleashed more questions than I could bear. So, I did what so many trauma survivors do; I buried it.

From that point on, I became a master at pretending.

I became the cheerful one. The positive one. The 'life of the party'. I sparkled. I smiled. I showed up in every room with a can-do attitude that deflected suspicion and invited admiration.

Underneath, I was breaking.

It's exhausting to live as a character you've created for survival.

Fast-forward several years, I was married to a beautiful man, pregnant with our third child and preparing to immigrate from the UK to Australia. Everything looked idyllic. A picture-perfect family on the cusp of a great adventure.

Then our son was born. And the facade collapsed.

What started as fog became a storm. I found myself swallowed by postnatal depression. And this time, I couldn't pretend. I couldn't keep the mask in place.

I remember sobbing in the doctor's waiting room, completely unrecognisable to myself. I had always prided myself on being strong, resourceful, in control. But now? I couldn't hold it together in front of strangers.

The lowest point came while driving. Overcome with emotional pain, I had a fleeting thought, *What if I just turned the wheel into the truck in oncoming traffic?*

That thought scared me. But the sound of my newborn son's gurgle in the back seat brought me back. That tiny noise was enough to ignite the maternal instinct that saved me; protect, not perish. I pulled over and cried like I never had before.

That was my turning point.

I reached out for help – for the third time in my life. And each time, it felt harder. The shame grew heavier. I knew what to do. I was trained in healing, self-awareness, trauma-informed approaches. I had helped others transform their lives. And yet, I was drowning in my own pain.

I remember trying to explain it to my father. 'But, Cathy,' he said, 'you have everything – a loving husband, beautiful children, a lovely home. Why are you depressed?'

He didn't mean harm. He simply didn't understand. And that's what makes emotional illness so brutal. You know you should be happy. You see your blessings. But you can't feel them. The guilt of that gap can be soul-crushing.

Then came the next wave.

Each of our five children – our extraordinary, sensitive, beautiful children – were diagnosed as neurodivergent.

I cried each time. Not because I wished they were different but because I knew their path would be harder. I knew the world wouldn't always see their brilliance. I knew they would need strength, stability and self-assuredness from me – and I wasn't sure I had it.

That realisation shook me to my core; *as I was, I wasn't the parent they needed.*

So I went back into the fire. I dug deeper. I faced the pain I hadn't yet touched. I began training in trauma, not just to serve others, but to finally, truly, heal myself.

I made a vow: *the pain ends with me.*

No more passing down silent wounds. No more inherited suffering disguised as strength. No more pretending.

I would break the cycle.

Working with highly successful clients, seven-figure business owners, media personalities, CEOs, I began to notice a pattern.

On the surface, they had it all. But behind the scenes, many were falling apart. Their achievements had become a smokescreen for unaddressed pain.

Trauma doesn't vanish when you hit your goals. It just waits for quiet moments to rise again.

Here are the truths I've come to believe, both professionally and personally:

1. *Trauma isn't what happens to you – it's how your system receives it.* You can live through horror and be resilient or experience something seemingly small and be shattered. I once worked with a woman who had survived years of abuse, but the memory that held the most emotional charge? A teacher humiliating her in Year 5. The nervous system chooses what it holds onto. It doesn't follow logic. It follows emotion.
2. *Big T or little t – it doesn't matter.* The nervous system reacts the same. You either feel safe, or you don't. And if you don't, you learn to adapt in ways that protect you – but also limit you.
3. *Minimizing your pain may keep you functioning – but you are never free.* So many people say, 'It wasn't that bad,' or 'Others have it worse.' But healing doesn't come from comparison, it comes from permission

– to feel, to speak, to acknowledge.
4. *Success without healing is a trap.* So many leaders use their trauma as rocket fuel but when they reach the top, they wonder why they still feel empty. Success doesn't erase trauma. It amplifies what's unresolved.
5. *Most people are stuck in survival mode.* Fight. Flight. Freeze. Fawn. We make decisions, build relationships, raise children and run businesses from a dysregulated state. No wonder the world feels chaotic. Healing our nervous systems isn't just personal – it's cultural.

From all of this – my breakdowns, breakthroughs and bold choices – *The Backyard Peace Project* was born.

A global movement built on the belief that world peace begins in our own backyards. It begins in homes like mine and yours. In everyday choices. In inner work and outer impact.

It began with a vision; to create a soft place to land. A place where people could heal. Belong. Be seen. Be held. Be real.

Now it's a vibrant global community offering:
- Trauma-informed coaching.
- Masterclasses and healing sessions.
- Monthly summits with global thought leaders.
- Peer support and connection.
- Resources to help people reclaim their wholeness.

It's affordable. Accessible. And deeply, radically transformative.

It's not about fixing people, it's about remembering who we are beneath the pain.

It's about choosing peace, not just as a wish, but as a practice.

This journey – my personal walk through fire – has made me the mother, the mentor, the woman and the leader I am today.

I've stood in the trenches of trauma. I've collapsed in the arms of grief. I've questioned my sanity, my strength, my worth. And I've come through with a knowing that cannot be shaken:

The power to choose is the most sacred gift we hold.

We cannot always control what happens. But we can choose how we respond.

We can choose to seek help. To tell the truth. To speak gently to ourselves.

To unlearn what doesn't serve us.

To reach out, even when we want to hide.

It's a choice.

My mission is simple:

To equip, support and love people as they become the most healed, whole and powerful versions of themselves.

Because world peace isn't some far-off fantasy.

It begins with inner peace.

It begins in our homes, in our relationships, in our nervous systems.

It begins with a parent choosing to heal so their children don't inherit their pain.

It begins with a leader choosing vulnerability instead of perfection.

It begins with you.

It begins with me.

It begins in our backyards.

And it begins with the power to choose.

If you take anything from my story, let it be this:

You are not broken. You are becoming.

You are not behind. You are awakening.

You are not alone. You are part of something bigger.

You have the power to choose.

And in choosing yourself, you change everything.

And most of all – we can choose to break the cycle.

To anyone reading this who's carrying more than they let on:

I see you.

CATHY DOMONEY

I know what it's like to perform while you're in pain.
To give while feeling empty.
To help others while wondering who's helping you.
You're not alone.
You're not broken.
And you have the power to choose again. And again. And again.
Choose peace.
Choose truth.
Choose love.
Choose rest.
Choose you.
You don't have to have it all together. You just have to begin.
Because peace isn't a place you find – it's a path you walk.
And every single step is a choice.
World peace is possible.
It starts with us, in our own backyards.

ABOUT CATHY

An expert with over twenty years of experience in teaching, counseling, hypnotherapy, cutting-edge trauma release techniques and coaching, bestselling author Cathy Domoney specializes in working with high-achievers, including seven-figure entrepreneurs, to dissolve their blocks, triggers and trauma hindering their true greatness. Her focus on empowering high-performance entrepreneurs and professionals through innovative techniques and technologies underscores her commitment to unlocking their infinite potential, leading them to experience more love, impact, legacy, successS and financial wealth.

CHRISTOPHER KAI
THE SALES SPELL

'In the past ten years, this man has built a following of entrepreneurs in the millions. He's co-founded the software company ClickFunnels that has gone to over $100 million and 55,000 customers in just three years. Ladies and gentlemen, bring to the stage with a thunderous 10X applause – Mr Russell Brunson.'

This is how entrepreneur Russell Brunson was introduced at a business conference called 10X organized by Grant Cardone. Brunson is little known in the mainstream business world but he has Brad Pitt-notoriety in the online marketing and personal development space. He co-founded a billion-dollar valued SAAS company called ClickFunnels. That day when he walked on stage, he gave a ninety-minute keynote. He walked off stage making $3 million.

You heard that right: $3,000,000 from one ninety-minute speech.

To put it in context, I am a Fortune 100 global speaker represented by ten speaking bureaus in five countries. At the time of this book printing, I charge five figures for an hour-long corporate keynote speech. That's considered the top 1% of corporate speakers in the world. US President George W Bush's reported speaker fee is $100,000.

How can a little-known online marketing guy make thirty times more than a president of the United States of America?

The simple answer is – Russell Brunson is a wizard of words and a master at stage sales in the personal development space.

He has perfected what I call the '3 Story Sales Close' strategy.

CHAPTER PURPOSE

In this chapter, you will learn this three story sales close strategy that Russell has used to make $3 million from one speech and $100 million in three years. This is the same three story sales close strategy that all successful wizard of words like Elon Musk, Oprah Winfrey or Jeff Bezos use to start and scale their billion-dollar brands.

You will also learn the business side of speaking so you understand how to monetize your message, five proven science-based persuasion strategies, and the one secret power you have that will exponentially help you become a wizard of words in sales.

THE BUSINESS SIDE OF SPEAKING (HOW TO MONETIZE YOUR MESSAGE)

Cherilyn Castlemann is a senior corporate executive with decades of sales experience with Fortune 500 firms. A few years ago, she was a guest on my *Gifters* podcast where she shared tips and strategies on how to be better at sales. When I told her about what I did, how I get to travel the world first class as a corporate speaker, help people by sharing stories, and am compensated very well for it – all the while meeting some of the most inspiring people – I remember her response to me when I asked her,

'Cherilynn, have you ever considered being a corporate speaker? You have an inspiring story and years of relevant corporate sales experience. You'd be great!' Her response, 'I'm intrigued.'

She ended up signing up for our GPS speaker training online program and she is now consistently booking speeches and consultant projects with Fortune 100 companies. Cherilynn is getting paid as a corporate speaker.

There are three basic ways to make a living from being a speaker:

1. Corporate stages (get paid before you step on stage).
2. Other people's stages (get paid after you step on stage).
3. Your own stages (get paid before and after you step on stage).

CORPORATE STAGES

I used to work at American Express on Wall Street as a business strategist. Most large global firms want to always stay current and relevant so they will either organize conferences for their employees or they will pay for their employees to attend conferences or training. I remember I attended a Dale Carnegie seminar paid for by my employer because it was considered career development.

What you may not realize is the conference and events industry is a $1 trillion industry and the biggest portion of that is in corporate conferences and seminars. That alone is a $300 billion industry. Any time you attend a conference, they will always have a roster of speakers. You might think that, why would anyone hire you to speak? That's what I thought too when I first began, but if you have a specific knowledge and you craft your message is a compelling way – you can get paid as a keynote speaker. That's why I created GPS, an online speaker training program to help my clients do just that.

If you attend conferences, take a look at the roster of speakers. If you objectively ask yourself, 'Were all of them good?' Probably not. Do you think you can add more value than some of those speakers? If the answer is yes, then you should consider speaking at those conferences rather than attending them.

In the corporate world of speaking, they pay you upfront. Usually, they will pay you 50% upfront which is non-refundable and the remaining balance on the day of your speech. That also doesn't include travel expenses which you should always ask for and you can also sell them your books. So, when you are a corporate speaker, you really have three sources of income – the corporate speaker fee, travel expense allowance and book sales.

Speaking for corporate conference, however, is the hardest form of monetizing your message since you really need to have a speaker website, a clear keynote description, ideally a speaking reel and various forms of social proof that you are an expert in your field. Writing a book, being featured in international publications like *Forbes* and procuring prominent testimonials from recognizable names in your industry or the world will improve your chance of booking new stages.

For instance, you may not know me, but I wrote a number-one international bestselling book about networking with billionaires. One of the topics my clients hire me for is on how to master business networking. At one point, I interviewed billionaire visionary Elon Musk and during our interview he said to me, 'Wow! You really know a lot!' Whether you know me or not, if the richest man in the world and *Time* magazine's 'Most Influential Person' says that I know a lot, it conveys to you that I have authority and knowledge.

OTHER PEOPLE'S STAGES

Speaking on other people's stages – that aren't large corporations – is easier than convincing a corporation to hire you. When you speak at these events they may not have a budget to hire you but if you have consultant services or coaching programs, you can speak in front of their large audience, and have the highest probability of meeting your clients in the audience.

Why attend an event when you can be speak at the same event. Don't just be a guest in a sea of a thousand people. Be the speaker on stage in front of a thousand people. That's why speaking is the best form of sales. Speaking is what I call 'next-level networking'. You meet the speakers the most important people at the conference and those are the VIP and speakers you meet in the green room behind the stage. Your audience, prospects and clients all immediately see you as an authority. I call it 'instant and unquestionable credibility'. No one will ever question your credibility when you are a speaker.

In this approach you may not get paid on the front end, but if you research the audience and have a consultant service or coaching program, you can make more on the back end selling your programs than if you were hired to be a paid speaker. I recently met Neil Patel, a *New York Times* bestselling author. *Forbes* endorsed 'Top 10 Marketers' and recognized as one of the top hundred entrepreneurs under the age of thirty by President Obama. He mentioned how though he can command a five-figure speaker fee, he has offered to speak regardless of the speaker fee because he knows that if he's in the right audience, he can make seven to eight figures in consultant fees when he follows up with his prospects from that audience.

CREATE YOUR OWN STAGE

The last way you can make money as a speaker is to create your own stage – your own event. It can be in-person, virtual or a hybrid of both. I remember I recently gave a virtual keynote for one of my corporate banking clients in the morning at my hotel room in Columbus, Ohio. Then, at night, I speak at an in-person event for a real estate community where I invited them to attend one of my own trainings on how to 'Master Networking in a Day'.

You might think you need a lot of capital and a big budget, but you don't when you are first starting off. One of my clients is named Shelly. She describes herself as 'The Grandma From Idaho'. Shelly grew up on a farm in Washington and eventually moved to Idaho. With just two events, I helped her make close to $100,000. When I asked her husband what he thought after the first event, he said, 'You should do this every day.' (If you were in the corporate world earning that in one day you'd need to be a celebrity or US president.)

Six figures in one day is twice as much as the average American earns in a year. And, the first event only had ten guests and the second event only had nine guests. I had one other client in Columbus, Ohio, where I helped him generate $20,000 from a three-hour training with only three people in the room. You start adding these five- and six-figure payouts and you are well on your way to becoming a millionaire.

The way I helped her generate six figures came down to a business model for speakers that is well known in the personal development space. It's called the 'speak to sell' model. You speak on stage (in-person or virtually) either for free or a low-priced entrance ticket, and then at the end of your presentation, you upsell them your program, coaching or consultant services.

When you create your own stage, you get both paid on the front end from ticket sales and on the back end with your upsells. After the initial event, you will generate even more revenue when you keep helping and serving your clients and through intentional follow up with existing clients that five or six figures will eventually grow into seven and eight figures if you stay the course and always remember how you can add more value to your clients' lives. In Russell Brunson's case, I recently attended one of his events where you made $20 million from that one event and $100 million in just three years in business. This is how Tony Robbins has made billions over the years.

DON'T DO THIS

Don't do what I did when I first started my speaking career. I was completely unaware and very skeptical about the personal development space.

I remember giving a speech in Beverly Hills regarding my book, *Big Game Hunting: Networking with Billionaires, Executives and Celebrities*. An entrepreneur named Asko who was from Estonia walked up to me and said, 'I love your speech and your book. What's your program?' I literally looked at him dumbfounded and responded, 'What do you mean?' I had no clue what he was talking about until I dove in and started learning about how the self-help, personal development space actually makes money. An 'online program' is how Tony Robbins, the king of self-help, and the vast majority of the self-help industry – generate their revenue.

UPSELLS ARE THE 9TH WONDER OF THE WORLD

Billionaire investor Warren Buffett often loves to talk about how compound interest is the eighth wonder of the world. If he knew about the speak-to-sell model, he would realize that 'upsells' would be the ninth, tenth, eleventh wonders of the world.

Every single successful company has a 'upsell' product because you can generate two to nine times your revenue on the backend. Even established brand like Uber or American Airlines offer upsells. You book a regular Uber ride, they immediately upsell you to UberLux. 'For only $7.88 more, you can ride in a more comfortable luxury car.' You book an economy ticket on American Airlines and a day later, you get an email saying, 'Do you want to upgrade to business class to experience these added benefits?'

The personal development space has perfected this speak-to-sell upsell model and has helped many experts to become millionaires and multimillionaires. This 'upsell' approach is how Russell Brunson made $3 million in one speech. He spoke for free but then after his ninety-minute speech, you offer an online program where the audience bought it. I attended his recent annual event called Funnel Hack Live and then he made $6 million from ticket sales on the frontend and I heard he made an additional $14 million on the backend selling a five-figure online package. That's $20 million revenues from one event. Do you know what I call that? I call that 'hedge fund money'.

Upsells are great because you can teach a free class and then once your attendees learn from you and after the end of your speech if they want to learn more from you, they can make investments in your paid services or online programs. It's the best approach to service. You give a little and then you ask if they want to learn more.

There are no more excuses NOT to have a side hustle when you understand and apply to speak to sell upsell model. You can create a coaching program on a free website called canva.com, use Zoom to deliver the content, all in the comforts of your own home.

You don't need a college degree from a fancy school. You don't need a marketing budget when you first start off. You don't need connections. You just need be a burning desire to live a better life and be motivated enough to learn a new skill set of sales and online marketing. That same client who I helped generate six figures is a mother of five, a grandma and she grew up on a farm. She is an inspiration to anyone who thinks being an entrepreneur is only for the few select.

What's the alternative? Working at a day job that pays you a salary, where even if you had the best promotion in the world, you will always be capped out at a certain level. You never want to just have a day job where you can't exponentially increase your income or revenue. I have dozens of GPS speaker and coaching clients that all have day jobs but they are choosing to create a side hustle as a speaker and online coach so they can attain their own financial freedom.

'Outsized returns often come from betting against conventional wisdom. Given a 10% chance of a hundred times payoff, you should take that bet every time.' – Jeff Bezos

THE 3 STORY SALES CLOSE STRATEGY

I have taught this strategy to 100,000s of individuals in 92 countries. It works anywhere with anyone because it is based on fundamental human principles of connection, science, and storytelling. It has been especially helpful for my GPS speaker clients who are entrepreneurs and professionals who want to understand how to create and scale a speaking and online coaching business.

The 3 foundational stories you must master in sales are:
1. A personal story so your clients can *Relate* to you.
2. A professional story so your clients can *Aspire* to be you.
3. A client story so they have a reason why they should *Pay* you.

Donald is a 29-year-old real estate executive based in Columbus, Ohio. When we first met, he expressed interest in being a speaker and online coach. At first, he signed up for our GPS speaker training group coaching program where we teach our clients the business side of speaking. We teach our clients how to define your expertise, market your expertise, and get paid for your expertise (even if you think you're not an expert or you feel like an imposter.)

Once he got a taste of our group coaching, he decided he wanted to accelerate his progress so he invested in one of our more premium 'Concierge VIP in a Day' services where we do a deep dive into how we can create the foundation of his speaking and coaching business in one day.

I set up a private meeting area in an exclusive club in Beverly Hills and when Donald arrived he was ready to get to work. I walked him through exactly how he can create a speaker and coaching program from scratch. And, the large bulk of our day was defining his 3 stories he would use to present himself. I helped him piece together his entire personal, professional, and client stories.

His personal story is both inspiring and heartbreaking. At a nine-year-old bright-eyed kid, he was excited to play in little league football. But as soon as he went to tryout, his coach pulled him aside and said, 'Hey kid, you need to weigh yourself. If you are over 99 pounds, we will need to put a red sticker on your helmet.'

How Donald translated this was, 'Hey nine-year-old Donald. You're a fat kid and even though you're self-conscious about your weight, we are going to make sure every single person on your team also knows that you are fat.' This 'label' stuck with Donald well through his school years and even into his mid 20s.

If affected adversely affected his self-esteem, his self-image, and his ability to make friends and meet girls. He never dated anyone in high school because he never felt confident enough to approach a girl. 'Why would they like this "fat" guy?', he thought. At one point he ballooned to 250 pounds.

It was more than 10 years after that 'red sticker' label that he had a breakdown. In his early 20s, where he had just started as a real estate agent working part-time. he also had a another job as a nurses aide where he would care for patients with disabilities. One such patient was a man named Keith. When Keith relieved himself, he wasn't able to clean himself. So Donald, put on his gloves and every single day for an entire day, Donald would literally have to scoop chunks of feces from underneath Keith every day he defecated on himself.

'I couldn't believe my life turned out like this,' Donald recalls. 'I'm fat, lonely, and depressed, and now I'm literally scooping up someone's crap.' At that point, he was determined to turn his life around with his health and his wealth.

All through out his 20s, he was determined to be successful. He began focusing on being a great real estate agent. Then he started investing in real estate properties, buying and flipping homes, and eventually buying his own home by the time he was 29. In 10 years, he has made $100 million in real estate transactions and helped his clients make millions in real estate investments. At that point, his community started seeing his results, and they started asked him for advice.

He would eventually start coaching and he has since helped them make millions in real estate investments. One such client named Solomon was only 19 when he met Donald. By the time he was 21 he was already a millionaire thanks to Donald's advice. 'If it wasn't for Donald's advice, I definitely would not be so successful,' exclaimed Solomon.

3 STORY BREAKDOWN

You just read Donald's personal, professional, and client stories? Was his 'personal' story relatable to you? Have you ever felt like someone 'labeled' you and said you were too fat, too short, too dumb, too tall, too thin, too weird, too smart, or too different?

Then you read about his professional story. If you wanted to learn how to invest in real estate, doesn't his 10 years of real estate experience with $100 million in transactions make you want to aspire to be him?

Don't you want to be a millionaire? It's less about the money but the 'time freedom' and piece of mind you have when you know you can pay your bills on time, you don't have to stress about finances, and you're not always worried about any surprise expenses that pop up in your life.

The client story is most especially important in sales. According to McKinsey, they released a 'Consumer Decision Journey' Report, and found that 31% of your sales success came down to what they called 'consumer-driven marketing.' Simply put, it doesn't matter what Donald says about how great he is as a coach. His clients, his 'consumer-driven' testimonials are the best form of marketing.

This 3 story sales close works in any industry. You look at someone like Elon Musk. If you watch his YouTube videos, you learn about his personal story:

1. He grew up in Pretoria, South Africa where he was a bullied to the point of being hospitalized. Raised with a single mom, estranged from his father. (Relatable)
2. He comes to America, starts a few companies, sells them and becomes a multi-millionaire. (Aspirational)
3. Tesla customer testimonials. I have never met a Tesla customer who doesn't rave about how much they love their Tesla. (Reason to buy)

THE BEST SALES PEOPLE IN THE WORLD ARE WIZARDS OF WORDS

Warren Buffett isn't known as a salesperson but he is one of the best. It's one thing to sell someone a product or service but in his 20s as a little known investor with a minimum track record, he convinced others to invest their money with the hope of getting a return on investment.

Oprah Winfrey isn't known as a salesperson but after decades of dominating the media industry with her Oprah Winfrey Show, how do you think she did it? She's a brilliant Wizard of Words who understands how to give her audience what they want.

Every single 'successful person' you can think about whether in the business world or otherwise were either brilliant sales people who had the media machine to sell you on who they were or what they do. From Gandhi to Mandela, Kennedy to Churchill, Jesus Christ to Buddha, the media has sold us on the fact that these individuals are visionaries.

Find out more here:

ABOUT CHRISTOPHER

Christopher Kai is the founder and CEO of The Mathem Group, a Beverly Hills-based leadership and sales training firm. He is one of the world's leading authorities in story-based leadership, a Fortune 100 global speaker, number-one global bestselling author and founder of GPS, the premier speaker training program in the world with clients in 120 cities, twenty-nine countries and six continents. He is a former business strategist and executive speechwriter at American Express. Elon Musk once exclaimed during an interview, 'Wow, you really know a lot.'

His clients include: Google, American Express, Discover, New York Life, Merrill Lynch, Farmers Insurance, Bank of America, and the U.S. Consulate. He has authored five books, has been featured on CNN, ABC News, BuzzFeed, Fast Company and Forbes and is a former Huffington Post contributor.

His four main keynotes are about: 1. Story-based Leadership 2. Team Building 3. Story-based Sales Mastery and 4. Elevate Your Business Relationships. He has also given keynotes for colleges, universities and non-profits. All of his keynotes are based on his twenty years of global experience and exhaustive research. Outside of his business, he founded Mondays at the Mission, the only homeless youth program of its kind in the world at Union Rescue Mission, the largest private shelter in the U.S. They have helped thousands of homeless students stay in school, find jobs and attend college. Their esteemed speakers list include: Grammy and Oscar winners, FBI agents, Navy Seals, Olympians and astronaut Buzz Aldrin, world record-holding swimmer Diana Nyad and business visionary Elon Musk.

DEBORAH DICKINSON
BRAVE ENOUGH TO BEGIN AGAIN

Sometimes the bravest thing we can do is let go of who we think we should be and begin again as who we truly are. This chapter is my journey back to myself – a story of grief, courage, and rediscovering the purpose that was within me all along.

EMBRACE YOUR PAST WITH PURPOSE

'Absolutely, leave it in my capable hands,' I assured with a steady firmness, prompting the exchange of data files through the IT department. As I concluded one call, I promptly initiated another, urgency exuding through my voice, 'Caine, gather the team. I'm sending over the files now. We need to reprocess them and get them down to the print room … yesterday.'

As I swung open the door to the print room, the immediate recognition in Mark's eyes told me he sensed the gravity of my unexpected visit. It was far from a mere social call. 'Stop the presses!' I commanded, my voice cutting through the humming of high-speed printing machinery. 'Shred the 150,000 prints. New files are on their way – and, Mark, time is a luxury we don't have.'

With the crisis averted and the project back on track, I returned to my office, my stride quickening with the thrill of resolution. I updated my client, painting the picture of control regained. As I put down the phone and slumped back in the chair, the quiet of the evening started to settle around me. Swinging around in my chair, I high-fived an invisible hand in the air. *I love this job* I shouted loudly in my head, revelling in the satisfaction of a challenge met and an extremely pleased client.

Yet, even in that moment of victory, a fleeting thought whispered at the back of my mind: *Is this really all there is?* The thrill of problem-solving, of being in control, was intoxicating … but was I leading or was I just surviving.

This was just another chapter in my corporate saga, a testament to the deep-seated passion that had propelled me through my career. My days were filled with success, strong client relationships and a vibrant social circle. I was scaling the corporate ladder, each rung securely climbed taking me higher on that ladder.

My journey began in a small, idyllic town in New Zealand, where my childhood was surrounded by nature. A spirited, free little girl, I found joy in the simplicity of climbing trees, exploring waterfalls and running through the fields and paddocks, high on life with the sheer beauty and freedom that embraced me. However, one sun-filled day, tragedy struck. That night, after dad had left for work, friends in need appeared at our door, their car having broken down. My mother, forever the helper, drove to help them and I tagged along. It was a dark, still night, so I lost sight of her just before a harsh bright light appeared, followed by a deafening bang. In that instant, she was gone, her life stolen by a drunk driver. My world shattered, plunging into darkness, grief and fear. At just eleven, I was lost in a tumultuous sea of sorrow.

In that moment, I became my own leader. I didn't recognise it at the time, but the resilience that would carry me through the decades ahead was born that night. The years that followed were marked with turmoil. At fifteen, I fled from the remnants of my childhood home. By sixteen, I was a mother. By seventeen, a wife, and then divorced at nineteen. At twenty-one, I sought a fresh start in Australia, but the struggle persisted.

Job hopping, transient relationships and alcohol becoming a fleeting solace.

Life began to shift when I landed a job that would transition me from the factory floor to corporate heights, eventually ascending to the role of general manager. Yet, just as I settled into this new chapter, the ghost of doubt emerged. I wasn't unfamiliar with this state as it has visited me many times before. Tasked with devising a business plan amid talks of selling or shutting the business down, I felt overwhelmed with uncertainty and the realisation of how expendable I was.

Doubts clouded my mind, overshadowing the accolades I had once received for my composure and leadership. A persistent internal monologue haunted me, questioning my future and my worth. Was my identity merely tied to the corporate world? Had I built my confidence on being the go-to problem-solver, instead of on who I truly was?

Angela Duckworth, social psychologist, author of *Grit: The Power of Passion and Perseverance,* identifies the single quality that marks those who succeed in life; *understanding that personality and character are not fixed but can be shaped and strengthened by difficult experiences.* My experiences had made me strong, but had I allowed them to define my limits?

I grappled with the realisation that I was really just a commodity in the world of print and variable data of the corporate world I had lived for the last twenty-two years. In this spiralling vortex, I found myself repeatedly questioning, *What now? What am I truly good at? Can I really start over?* The echoes of these questions lingered, challenging the very essence of my drive and desire, my passion, my purpose.

'You may not control all the events that happen to you, but you can decide not to be reduced by them.' – Maya Angelou

ELEVATE RAISING YOUR STANDARDS – PURPOSE TO PASSION

As I stepped into the open, well-lit hotel foyer, the plush carpet seemed to rise, greeting my feet with each step forward. The rhythmic movement lifted the corners of my lips into an ever-widening smile, as epiphany struck. The weight of my past was suddenly dissolved, replaced by a buoyant lightness, each of my five senses tingling with the awareness of the moment. It was a transformative breakthrough – a seismic shift in my very being. With a profound certainty, I knew I was going to be okay! My past, once a shadow, had become my superpower.

Returning to Melbourne, now with a purpose-driven passion, I outlined my plan. The transition from salaried employee to audacious entrepreneur was clear:

- Step one, secure finances.
- Step two, establish a time frame.
- Step three, find my tribe.

Networking was foreign territory. In my corporate life, connections were made through necessity. But in the entrepreneurial world, I had to earn my place in rooms filled with strangers. The first networking event I attended, I hesitated outside the venue for several minutes before stepping inside. *Would they take me seriously? Did I even belong here?*

But the more I spoke, the more I realised I wasn't just another ex-corporate professional searching for purpose, I was someone with a story, with resilience, with leadership instincts honed through years of navigating uncertainty.

Throughout these interactions, I encountered mentors and peers who provided invaluable insights. Three pieces of advice resonated deeply, guiding me at critical junctures of my journey:

1. Be still and know that I am God. This proved to be profound as I was never really a religious person, but for me, somehow, I knew what it meant.
2. Get off your own agenda. This fits anything and everything in life. There are three types of people you will meet: those you learn from, those who need to learn from you, and those who are merely passing

through.

3. I am never surprised when one or more of these spring into mind, as I know it delivers a clear message to me at the time I need to be reminded.

Embracing my past, I now had to be committed to elevating my standards and consciously creating my desired reality. My journey aligned me with passionate causes and individuals whose values resonated with mine. I dove headfirst into these ventures, fuelled by admiration for the founders' drive and passion. This involvement not only expanded my horizons but enriched my knowledge immensely; experiences I would have missed had I not ventured beyond my comfort zone.

However, a familiar pattern emerged, drawing me back to the constraints and routines of an employee. My time became scarce, my passions sidelined, and I hovered on the brink of burnout. Shadows of self-doubt and unworthiness crept in, yet this time, I recognised them. Armed with resilience and a profound self-honesty, I acknowledged my deviation from the path I had set for my desires. Embracing this realisation, it was time to elevate myself. Decisions had to be made – for me.

Despite my deep involvement with the dreams of others, I realised I had yet to fulfil my own. It was time to return to my passion, my purpose.

'The greatest gift you can give yourself is the permission to be yourself.'
– Jim Rohn

EMERGE DELIBERATELY LIVING YOU – PASSION AND PURPOSE

I find myself standing in a dark room, the door is slightly ajar just letting in enough light to make out I am not alone. But I am not afraid. Strangely, I feel safe, as if I know this place; it's familiar. I can just make out a silhouette in the middle of the room, on the floor. I make my way towards it; my heart is thumping and tears are starting to well in my eyes. I reach out my hand to this little girl curled up on the floor. She looks up at me, smiles and nods, and with a loving look, receives my hand in hers. We lock eyes briefly as I pull her up off the floor, giving her a big warm embrace and kiss on the cheek. I tell her, 'Thank you for bringing us this far. You have silently created the shields of protection you believed we needed in all those moments, but I can take it from here …'

You see you never know how brave, how strong and how confident you can be until you begin to look inside. But I could feel it. There was something missing, something still incomplete. That question, *What are you passionate about?* no longer weighs me down. Instead, it urges me forward, a beacon guiding me toward my truth. I knew what I had to do next.

I go to my spot; the one spot in the house where I am alone and can stare out the window into the trees, listening to the birds. I let my thoughts jump from a little girl to who I am now, to who I see I could be. I don't question my thoughts, my visions, I just let it happen to see where it takes me:

The final bell for school sounds, as we all pack up and I run outside, go to the far fence to collect my towel and swimming togs. I love my new swimming togs, they are my favourite, bright and colourful, the orange standing out the most. Yay, it always feels exciting, the end of the school day, then suddenly Mrs Miller is tapping me on the shoulder, 'Excuse me, young girl. Those are not your togs. Give them to me and you go back to get your real ones.' I was stunned, tears welling in my eyes. 'But these are mine. My mum bought them for me!' I cry. She shook her head. 'No, they're not. Tania said her togs are missing and you have taken them, now give them back.'

I don't remember if I had to hand them over, but what I do remember, is crying all the way home. When my mum saw me, she asked what was wrong, and the next thing I knew, we were in the car. As we reversed out of the driveway, she suddenly stopped. There was Mrs Miller at the paper store. My mum walked across the road with a piece of paper in her hand and spoke to the teacher.

In that moment I felt safe. My mother had reacted immediately to the injustice. Later, it turned out that Tania and I had the same togs, except she had worn different ones that day.

When the teacher accused me of taking someone's belongings (which was untrue), I was faced with two prejudices that day:
- Your parents can't afford these so they cannot be yours.
- I believe the *white* girl over you … the *brown* girl.

These sorts of interpretations were felt by many of us brown, poor children; we never spoke of it aloud, it was just the way things were. There were moments when we weren't the poor kids, especially when Mum and Dad bought you the best pair of swimming togs you had ever owned.

That moment never left me. I realised the power of having someone who will stand up for you. Now, that is exactly what I want to be for others. The one who stands, who advocates, who empowers. I want every child to discover their talents and dreams, and every woman and man to live deliberately aligned to their true identity.

> *'You don't have to be great to start, but you have to start to be great.'*
> – Zig Ziglar

What drives my purpose is knowing that each step I take gets me closer to being able to create the space that allows this to come to life. Of course, my heart is with the many children living in small country towns in New Zealand where communities are bound by shared struggles and shared dreams. Hence, when I started, my purpose was to impact two thousand people that will go on to impact their own two thousand people. A community of four million people with a similar desire; to live deliberately, to live their purpose and their passion. Four million also represents the estimated population of New Zealand, where my spirit was sparked, where my passion was ignited, fuelled by the freedom, love and safety that I felt in the arms of my mum and dad. You see I had to be brave, to allow myself to be aware of how strong and confident I was. And I had to do this from the inside. That's when I truly allowed the external warrior to let down her guard, to connect to a part of me I had not felt for a very long time. The feminine little girl, lying in a dark room holding space for my return.

Standing in that dark room, I reached out to my younger self. 'Thank you,' I whispered, pulling her into a warm embrace. 'You've been so brave, so strong.' For the first time, I truly embraced my past – not as something to escape, but as the foundation of my purpose.

Each challenge helped me grow, each setback taught me something new. I was no longer searching for my passion. I was living it.

And for the young ones, I wanted to share this message: *No matter how tough things may seem, you have the strength within you to overcome your obstacles.*

For those who have already walked many miles, I hope this reminds you that it's never too late to rediscover your passion and purpose. Together, we can embrace the magic of life and all its possibilities.

'What lies behind us and what lies before us are tiny matters compared to what lies within us.' – Ralph Waldo Emerson

ABOUT DEBORAH

Deborah Dickinson is a recognised mindset coach, speaker and transformational leader dedicated to helping career-driven women unlock their full potential and redefine success on their terms. With a background spanning corporate leadership, personal development and cultural empowerment, Deborah is the founder of Deliberately Living YOU, a high-level coaching program designed to help women break through limiting beliefs, align with their values and step into their power.

Her journey is one of profound transformation. Raised in New Zealand of Māori descent (Te Taangata whenua Aotearoa), Deborah's early years were filled with nature, beauty and freedom. However, at the age of eleven, a tragic accident took her mother's life, plunging her into grief, fear and insecurity. Over the years, she built emotional armour to survive – navigating teenage motherhood, early marriage and the corporate world – eventually climbing the ranks from factory floor to general manager in a male-dominated industry.

Despite outward success, Deborah felt unfulfilled, trapped by societal expectations and self-imposed limitations. A pivotal moment of self-reflection and deep personal work led her to dismantle the barriers she had built and reconnect with her true purpose. This journey became the foundation for her coaching methodology, which integrates neuroscience, leadership development and heart-centred practices to help others create lasting change in their lives.

Through her work, Deborah guides high-achieving women – entrepreneurs, executives and professionals – through a structured embrace, elevate, emerge framework. She empowers them to reclaim their confidence, master their mindset and create legacies of impact and fulfillment. Her programs, keynotes and workshops inspire individuals worldwide to break free from fear, claim their power and lead deliberate, abundant lives.

Her message is clear: Success without fulfilment is not success. Deborah's work ensures that ambitious women don't just climb mountains but climb the right mountains – aligned with their deepest values and aspirations.

EMMA WEAVER
BUILDING MENTAL WEALTH

Let's consider the importance of discussing a topic of immense importance – one that is central to our lives, our happiness and our capacity to thrive in an increasingly complex world. This topic is not about financial wealth, but rather a more profound and enduring form of wealth: mental wealth. The concept of mental wealth encompasses the state of our mental wellbeing, the richness of our inner life, and the resilience that we can draw upon in times of need.

We often hear about the need to cultivate financial wealth to ensure our security and happiness. But how often do we consider the wealth of our minds? How often do we tend to the vault that holds our thoughts, emotions and psychological resilience? Just as financial wealth requires regular deposits, wise investments and careful management, so too does our mental wealth. The more we invest in our wellbeing daily, the greater our mental wealth becomes, enabling us to withdraw from this vault when life's challenges demand resilience and strength.

Today, I will explore how we can incorporate daily practices to build and sustain mental wealth. We will delve into the concept of a 'mental wealth vault', a metaphor for the reservoir of resilience and wellbeing we cultivate over time. We'll also examine the five ways to wellbeing – — connect, learn, give, be mindful and be active – alongside the principles of the four agreements. Moreover, we'll discuss the critical idea that 'what we don't express, we repress', as articulated in the groundbreaking book *The Body Keeps the Score* by Dr Bessel van der Kolk.

As we navigate through this discussion, I want to highlight the overarching importance of maintaining our mental health and wellbeing all the time, not just in moments of crisis. By doing so, we can live our best lives, fully present, fully engaged, and fully alive.

THE CONCEPT OF MENTAL WEALTH

Before we delve into the practicalities, let us first understand what mental wealth truly means. Mental wealth is the sum total of our psychological resources – our emotional intelligence, our capacity for joy, our resilience in the face of adversity and our ability to maintain mental equilibrium. Unlike financial wealth, which can fluctuate with the market's whims, mental wealth is something we build from within, independent of external circumstances.

Imagine your mind as a vault – a secure place where you store your most valuable assets. These assets include your positive experiences, your knowledge, your skills, your emotional connections and your self-awareness. Every day, through your actions, thoughts and behaviours, you make deposits into this mental wealth vault. These deposits might be small, such as a moment of gratitude, a good conversation, or a new skill learned, but over time they accumulate, creating a substantial reserve of mental wealth.

Just as with financial wealth, the more you invest in your mental wealth vault, the more you have to draw upon when you need it. When life throws challenges your way – be it stress at work, a personal loss, or a global crisis like the COVID-19 pandemic – you can withdraw from this vault to support your resilience and wellbeing. This concept highlights the importance of continuous investment in our mental health, not just as a reactive measure, but as a proactive approach to living a fulfilling life.

DAILY PRACTICES FOR MENTAL WEALTH

Building mental wealth requires consistent effort and intentionality. It's about making daily deposits into our mental wealth vault, ensuring that we are not only surviving but thriving. The key to this lies in integrating wellbeing practices into our daily lives. These practices are not grand or time-consuming; rather, they are simple, manageable actions that, when done regularly, create a profound impact.

1. THE FIVE WAYS TO WELLBEING

Let us begin by exploring the five ways to wellbeing, a framework that has been widely adopted for its simplicity and effectiveness. These five actions – connect, learn, give, be mindful and be active – are evidence-based strategies that contribute to mental health and overall wellbeing.

Connect

Human beings are inherently social creatures. Our connections with others provide us with support, joy and a sense of belonging. Regularly connecting with others, whether through a meaningful conversation, spending time with loved ones, or simply smiling at a stranger, enriches our lives and strengthens our mental wealth. These connections are like the golden coins in our mental wealth vault – valuable and enduring.

Learn

Continuous learning keeps our minds sharp and engaged. It doesn't necessarily mean formal education, but rather an attitude of curiosity and openness. Learning a new skill, exploring a hobby or even understanding a new perspective can make a significant deposit into your mental wealth vault. Learning empowers us and increases our confidence, making us more resilient in the face of challenges.

Give

Acts of giving, whether big or small, are incredibly powerful. When we give – be it our time, our attention or our resources – we not only benefit others but also ourselves. Giving fosters a sense of purpose and enhances our connection with others. It's a way of enriching the communal aspect of our mental wealth vault, creating a shared reservoir of wellbeing that we can all draw upon.

Be Mindful

Mindfulness is the practice of being present in the moment, fully engaged with whatever we are doing. It is about observing our thoughts and feelings without judgment. Mindfulness helps us to reduce stress, increase self-awareness and improve our overall emotional health. When we are mindful, we make conscious deposits into our mental wealth vault, ensuring that our reserves are not depleted by the distractions and stresses of daily life.

Be Active

Physical activity is not just beneficial for our bodies; it is crucial for our minds as well. Exercise releases endorphins, which are natural mood lifters, and helps to reduce anxiety and depression. Regular physical activity is a vital deposit into our mental wealth vault, keeping our minds as well as our bodies in optimal condition.

2. THE FOUR AGREEMENTS

In addition to the five ways to wellbeing, I want to introduce you to the four agreements – a set of principles derived from the wisdom of the ancient Toltec civilization. These agreements, as described by Don Miguel Ruiz in his book of the same name, provide a powerful guide for maintaining mental wealth by shaping our thoughts and actions.

Be Impeccable with Your Word
Words have immense power. They can create beauty or cause harm. Being impeccable with your word means speaking with integrity, saying only what you mean and avoiding negative self-talk or gossip. When we are mindful of our words, we foster positive relationships and a healthy internal dialogue, making significant deposits into our mental wealth vault.

Don't Take Anything Personally
Many of us are quick to take things personally, allowing others' actions or words to affect our self-worth. But understanding that what others say and do is a reflection of their own reality, not ours, can protect our mental wellbeing. By not taking things personally, we prevent unnecessary withdrawals from our mental wealth vault, maintaining our emotional balance.

Don't Make Assumptions
Assumptions can lead to misunderstandings, unnecessary stress and conflict. Instead of assuming, we should seek clarity through communication. This principle helps us avoid the mental and emotional strain that assumptions often cause, preserving the wealth in our mental vault.

Always Do Your Best
This agreement encourages us to strive for our best in every situation, while recognising that our best will vary from day to day. By always doing our best, we build self-esteem and resilience, contributing consistently to our mental wealth. This principle also teaches us to accept ourselves and our efforts, reducing self-criticism and enhancing our mental wellbeing.

The Repercussions of Repression
Now, let us turn to an essential aspect of mental wealth – understanding

the impact of unexpressed emotions. There is a saying, 'What we don't express, we repress.' Repression occurs when we suppress our emotions, thoughts, or experiences, pushing them out of our conscious mind. While repression might offer temporary relief, the unaddressed emotions often resurface in more harmful ways, affecting our mental and physical health.

In *The Body Keeps the Score*, Dr Bessel van der Kolk explores how trauma and unexpressed emotions are stored in the body, leading to both mental and physical health issues. The book reveals how the body and mind are intricately connected, and how unresolved psychological issues manifest as physical symptoms. This insight underscores the importance of addressing our emotions and experiences rather than repressing them.

When we express our emotions, whether through talking, writing, or other forms of creative expression, we release the emotional charge associated with those experiences. This act of expression is a deposit into our mental wealth vault, as it frees up mental and emotional space, allowing us to function more effectively and healthily.

Conversely, when we repress our emotions, we are not only depleting our mental wealth but also jeopardising our physical health. Chronic repression can lead to anxiety, depression and even physical ailments like headaches, muscle tension and digestive issues. It's a reminder that our mental wealth is not just about positive deposits; it's also about avoiding withdrawals through unhealthy coping mechanisms.

BUILDING AND SUSTAINING MENTAL WEALTH

Maintaining mental wealth requires more than just sporadic efforts; it demands a consistent and proactive approach. Here are some additional strategies to ensure that your mental wealth vault remains full and ready for any challenges life might present.

1. SELF-CARE AS A PRIORITY

Self-care is often misunderstood as selfishness, but in reality, it is a crucial component of mental wealth. Taking time for yourself, whether through relaxation, hobbies or simply taking a break, is a way to recharge and make deposits into your mental wealth vault. Self-care ensures that you have the energy and mental clarity to face life's challenges.

2. BUILDING EMOTIONAL RESILIENCE

Resilience is the ability to bounce back from adversity.

We live in a world that often celebrates achievement, success and the relentless pursuit of excellence. High achievers are frequently lauded as the epitome of hard work, discipline and perseverance. However, behind the accolades and accomplishments, there lies an essential but often overlooked element that fuels sustained success – mental health and wellbeing.

Today, I want to discuss how high achievers look after their mental health and wellbeing, and why this practice is not just important, but crucial for long-term success. As we explore this topic, I will share relevant statistics that underscore the significance of mental health in achieving and maintaining peak performance.

THE IMPORTANCE OF MENTAL HEALTH FOR HIGH ACHIEVERS

High achievers are individuals who consistently perform at the top of their field, whether in business, sports, academia or the arts. They are driven by a desire to excel, often pushing themselves to their limits to reach their goals. However, the pursuit of excellence can come at a cost if mental health is neglected.

Mental health is not just about the absence of mental illness; it encompasses overall emotional, psychological and social wellbeing. It affects how we think, feel and behave, and it is fundamental to our ability to cope with stress, work productively and contribute to our communities. For high achievers, maintaining good mental health is essential for sustaining performance over the long term.

According to a study by the World Health Organization (WHO), depression and anxiety cost the global economy an estimated $1 trillion per year in lost productivity. This statistic highlights the impact of poor mental health on performance and success. High achievers, who often work in high-pressure environments, are particularly vulnerable to mental health challenges, including burnout, stress, and anxiety.

In fact, a survey by Deloitte found that 77% of professionals reported experiencing burnout at their current job. Moreover, the Harvard Business Review reported that high achievers are more prone to burnout due to their relentless drive and perfectionism. These statistics emphasise the critical need for high achievers to prioritise their mental health.

HOW HIGH ACHIEVERS LOOK AFTER THEIR MENTAL HEALTH

So, how do high achievers look after their mental health and wellbeing? The answer lies in intentional practices and habits that protect and enhance their mental and emotional resilience. Here are some key strategies that high achievers employ:

1. PRIORITIZING SELF-CARE

Self-care is the foundation of good mental health, and high achievers understand its importance. They make self-care a non-negotiable part of their routine, whether it involves regular exercise, adequate sleep, healthy eating or relaxation activities such as meditation or spending time in nature.

For example, Arianna Huffington, the founder of *The Huffington Post* and Thrive Global, is a strong advocate for the importance of sleep and self-care. After experiencing burnout herself, she has been vocal about how essential it is for high achievers to prioritise rest and recovery. The National Sleep Foundation recommends seven to nine hours of sleep per night for adults, yet many high achievers sacrifice sleep for work. However, studies show that sleep deprivation can impair cognitive function, decision-making and creativity – abilities that are crucial for high performance.

2. SETTING BOUNDARIES

High achievers are often ambitious and driven, which can lead to overwork and blurred boundaries between professional and personal life. However, those who sustain success over the long term recognise the importance of setting clear boundaries. This might mean establishing specific work hours, taking regular breaks or disconnecting from work-related technology during personal time.

A study published in the *Journal of Occupational Health Psychology* found that employees who regularly took short breaks throughout the day reported higher levels of job satisfaction and reduced levels of emotional exhaustion. High achievers who respect their own boundaries protect their mental health and ensure that they can maintain high performance without succumbing to burnout.

3. CULTIVATING EMOTIONAL INTELLIGENCE

Emotional intelligence (EQ) is the ability to understand and manage your own emotions, as well as the emotions of others. High achievers with high EQ are better equipped to handle stress, communicate effectively, and navigate the challenges of leadership and teamwork.

A study by TalentSmart found that 90% of top performers have high emotional intelligence, highlighting its importance in achieving success. These individuals are not only skilled at recognising their own emotional states but also at regulating their responses and maintaining a positive outlook even in challenging situations.

4. SEEKING SUPPORT

Despite their strengths, high achievers are not immune to the pressures and challenges of life. One of the most effective ways they protect their mental health is by seeking support when needed. This could involve talking to a trusted friend or mentor, consulting with a therapist or coach or joining a support group of like-minded individuals.

A report by the American Psychological Association (APA) shows that therapy and counselling are effective in reducing symptoms of depression, anxiety and stress. High achievers understand that seeking help is not a sign of weakness but a proactive step towards maintaining mental wellbeing.

5. PRACTISING MINDFULNESS AND STRESS MANAGEMENT

Mindfulness is the practice of being present in the moment and observing one's thoughts and feelings without judgment. High achievers use mindfulness techniques, such as meditation, deep breathing or journaling, to manage stress and maintain mental clarity.

A study by the American Psychological Association found that mindfulness meditation can reduce stress, improve focus and increase overall well-being. High achievers who incorporate mindfulness into their daily routines are better able to stay calm under pressure, make thoughtful decisions and maintain a balanced perspective.

6. CONTINUOUS LEARNING AND GROWTH

High achievers are lifelong learners who constantly seek opportunities for personal and professional growth. This mindset not only enhances their skills and knowledge but also contributes to their mental wellbeing by fostering a sense of purpose and fulfilment.

Research by Stanford University's Carol Dweck on the growth mindset shows that individuals who believe in their ability to grow and improve are more resilient and successful than those with a fixed mindset. High achievers who embrace a growth mindset are better equipped to handle challenges and setbacks, viewing them as opportunities for learning rather than as failures.

THE ROLE OF ORGANIZATIONS IN SUPPORTING MENTAL HEALTH

While high achievers take personal responsibility for their mental health, organizations also play a crucial role in supporting the wellbeing of their employees. Companies that prioritize mental health create an environment where high achievers can thrive without sacrificing their wellbeing.

A study by the World Economic Forum and Harvard School of Public Health found that for every $1 invested in treating common mental health issues, there is a $4 return in improved health and productivity. This statistic underscores the value of mental health programs in the workplace.

Organizations can support mental health by promoting work-life balance, offering mental health resources such as counselling or wellness programs, and fostering a culture of openness where employees feel comfortable discussing mental health issues without fear of stigma.

CONCLUSION

In conclusion, the path to sustained success is not solely paved with hard work and ambition; it is also built on the foundation of strong mental health and wellbeing. High achievers understand that to maintain peak performance over the long term, they must prioritize their mental health just as much as their professional goals.

By practising self-care, setting boundaries, cultivating emotional intelligence, seeking support, practising mindfulness and embracing continuous growth, high achievers not only protect their mental health but also enhance their capacity to achieve and sustain success.

As we continue to strive for excellence in our own lives, let us remember that mental health is not a luxury but a necessity. It is the cornerstone of true success – the kind that endures, enriches and empowers us to live our best lives.

ABOUT EMMA

Emma Weaver is the founder of Mental Wealth International, an organization supporting businesses to achieve better mental health and wellbeing within the workplace.

Emma is also an international bestselling author with her debut novel, *The Blue Line*.

An international speaker, Emma uses her voice to champion causes close to her heart. Her purpose in life is to support people to have a voice and to create a safe platform where this can happen.

Emma has over twenty-two years experience working in the mental health and wellbeing sector. Motivated by her purpose, Emma provides hope and expertise to people through both her personal and professional skills and experiences.

Emma currently resides in County Fermanagh, a beautiful rural county in Ireland. A native of Clones, Emma lives very close to her family homestead. She is a mother of three beautiful children, who are her world and her inspiration every day.

KABINGA MAZABA
ENDURANCE BEYOND THE STRIPES OF CHALLENGES

'Not everything that is faced can be changed, but nothing can be changed until it is faced.' – James Baldwin

Imagine standing at the starting line of the most unpredictable race you'll ever run – the race of life. It's not just a battle for survival, it's an electrifying rush to stay one step ahead, where that single step could mean the difference between triumph and oblivion. In this race, distractions are as abundant as the stars, weaving through our path, tempting us to veer off course. The race of life does not crown the swift, the battle does not favour the strong. Life is the mental marathon, set into motion from our first breath – a race where the swift-footed may falter, and the mightiest warriors may fall. The victory belongs not to the fastest or the strongest but to those who endure and remain authentic in the face of life's greatest trials. In this deafening journey, the twin forces of endurance and authenticity become our most prized allies.

But what is endurance and how does one keep their head above water when life hits hard from all corners? Let me define endurance using my life story.

SURVIVING THE UNBEARABLE
In my early childhood in Zambia, surrounded by a loving yet complex

extended family, I experienced both joy and pain. The freedom of my community, while liberating, exposed me to dangers, including sexual and emotional abuse. At six, my innocence was shattered by sexual abuse from my uncle, a trauma repeated at nine by a neighbor. When my parents discovered this, they kept it a secret, failing to seek justice or acknowledgement of my suffering due to cultural taboos, leaving me burdened with shame and feelings of unworthiness. My life was further marred by the loss of my father in a plane crash at eleven, followed by being publicly disowned by his family, immediately after he was put to rest. Following that, my mother's struggles as a single parent left me feeling emotionally abandoned and her untimely death deepened my sense of loss and pain, significantly shaping my outlook on life. My teenage years were far from easy, marred by low self-esteem, zero confidence, shame and suicidal ideations, with no self-belief. Unaddressed issues from my childhood cast long shadows into my adult life. However, through my journey of healing from trauma, I learned a profound truth: we don't choose our birth family or the twists and turns life throws our way. The unpredictability of life can leave deep scars, and trauma, often overwhelming, can strip away our sense of self and connection. Experiencing any form of abuse – be it emotional, physical or financial – shakes you to your core. It forces you to question everything about who you are and your worth. If endurance is the ability to withstand prolonged stressful hardship, then I embody that definition.

WARRIOR'S REBIRTH

Once you discover the truth within, you unlock the harmony of peace, allowing you to dance gracefully to the rhythm of your existence.

    The moment I tapped into the transformative power within through deep soul-searching, I began to redefine resilience from a warrior's perspective: to rise beyond the weight of my struggles. From this knowing, I had to muster the willpower to confront my deepest fear

– my childhood trauma. The fact that I had endured for many years to reach this critical point of realisation, I knew the time for change about the way I perceived life had arrived.

You see, for years, I wandered through a realm of denial, my past covered in silence, a story untold, believing it should remain hidden from the world. Embracing my truth was a journey marked with pain; from a tender age, I learned to bury my emotions and feelings deep within, my way of coping and enduring was to conceal my scars, to never reveal the depth of my experiences, for in my culture, voicing such truths was forbidden – fear of societal ridicule and the shame that came with it. The thought of sharing my story, shedding light on my darkest moments, was a bridge I never dared to cross. I found no refuge in silence and pretence from the relentless storm of pain and shame that followed my trauma. Haunted by the fear of judgement and the whispers of others, I longed for acceptance and belonging. However, revealing my soul seemed unthinkable.

Change is always a new territory to explore. And for so many years I resented change, anything that was not familiar to me was a no-go zone area. Realising that I had to take charge and face my challenges directly, I understood that no one else could resolve them for me. Sometimes, we look to others to fix our problems, but the truth is, the solutions lie within us. Delegating your life expectations to others often leads to more frustration and stagnation.

Facing myself honestly, even when uncomfortable, meant holding myself accountable, letting go of playing the victim, indulging in self-pity, making excuses, and clinging to limiting beliefs. Most importantly, I learned to forgive myself and those who harmed me. Forgiveness opened my heart to new beginnings, allowing emotional healing, the release of negative emotions, and a path to peace.

For change to take root, we must embrace our imperfections. This acknowledgment is powerful – it's our reason, our surrender to higher powers, our realisation that things must change. It drives us to aspire and grow. James Baldwin said, 'Not everything that is faced can be changed, but nothing can be changed until it is faced.' This holds true that while not everything in life can be transformed, acknowledging and facing our realities is the first step towards finding meaningful change. It can be said that a warrior gets rebirthed within first before affecting external matter.

Embracing the transformative power of change begins with authenticity. In the sacred space of honesty and self-awareness, we find our true essence. Only by courageously confronting our truths can we initiate meaningful change, holding the keys to our metamorphosis. Through the profound act of embracing our authentic selves, we set the winds of change in motion, embarking on the magnificent journey of self-realisation and growth.

I've learned that a true warrior perseveres, continually rising no matter how often life knocks them down. It takes genuine courage to venture into the unknown, facing uncertainties that teach us to trust ourselves and discover our strengths and weaknesses. Within each of us lies a power beyond our comprehension, a force that transcends our mental limits. We are beings of energy, capable of overcoming any challenge.

The truly exciting part of life's journey is that, no matter where you are in your growth and self-realisation, or what challenges you face, there is always more within you. The divine spark inside you holds immense potential for healing and overcoming obstacles. Your ability to thrive lies in tapping into this inner strength. But to unlock this potential, you must find the courage to confront your challenges and be honest with yourself. This is where true mastery begins.

ROAR WITHIN: MENTAL MARATHON

'The greatest glory in living lies not in never falling, but in rising every time we fall.' – Nelson Mandela

Imagine you're at the starting line of a marathon, full of energy and ready to start the race. But as you go on, it gets tough. You start to feel like you can't take it anymore. You're tired, maybe even feeling like giving up. However, you keep pushing forward, step by step. Just like a marathon, life has its ups and downs. You climb hills and go through valleys. Endurance is like running a marathon. The often quoted proverb by Phillip C McGraw, 'Life is not a sprint, it's a marathon,' has led me to realise the deeper significance of endurance, given that life is far from linear, evolving from complicated to complex. Life inevitably presents us with challenges that can sometimes feel overwhelming, yet the human body is capable of pushing through all the pain. I know this from experience – I faced tough challenges as a child, the kind no child should go through. Just as a runner requires resilience to navigate the ups and downs of a trail, I too needed to cultivate resilience to succeed in life. The only way to truly see and use this strength was to accept and acknowledge my challenges. That was how I could start to dissolve the shame and the feeling of being stuck that came with my past abuses. I learned that with each challenge, it unveils an opportunity for growth if you are willing to see the other side of life. It's never easy to face these challenges, but understanding that you have the strength within you to overcome them can make all the difference.

Endurance is more than just reaching the finish line; it's about personal growth along the way. As you face each challenge, you transform, becoming more self-aware and resilient. This journey helps you discover your true strengths and embrace your weaknesses. The power of endurance is in moving forward, no matter the obstacles, tapping into a deep-seated resolve. This not only builds resilience but also enriches your character, making each step of the journey worthwhile. Keep pushing through, and let endurance reveal your true potential.

Endurance requires focus and emotional strength to keep going, just like you need physical stamina to finish a long run. It introduces you to your most resilient self, not at the start, but near the finish line. This persistence is deeply connected to your vision and the significance of your dreams. To truly endure, you must anchor yourself in hope, faith and action, seeing even the faintest light at the end of the tunnel as a guide. As you overcome each obstacle, you don't just put back the broken pieces of your life; you rebuild yourself into someone stronger, someone transformed. Endurance positively shapes your character.

DISCOVERING YOUR AUTHENTIC SELF THROUGH CHALLENGES

Being part of the book series *Hear Us Roar* under the Siberian tiger theme, I was fascinated to learn what makes this particular tiger so unique compared to other animals. In my research, I discovered that Siberian tigers are known for their distinctive striped fur. Much like human fingerprints, where no two people have the same pattern, each Siberian tiger has its own unique set of stripes. This uniqueness among Siberian tigers, and the parallel similarity with human fingerprints, illustrates the concept of authenticity: every individual, whether tiger or human, is truly one-of-a-kind.

HOW DOES ONE FIND THEIR AUTHENTIC SELF?

Finding your authentic self involves a journey of self-discovery that requires introspection, honesty, and sometimes, vulnerability. To find my authentic self, I first had to shed off the victimhood I carried and begin to see things as they are. Understanding who I was and why I kept running away from myself. I had a deliberate difficult conversation with myself, and in order to start living as the real me. I made a conscious choice to define life values that truly represented who I was.

I recently read an article from *Harvard Business Review* titled 'How to

Find Your Values and Use Your Values'. It highlighted the immense power of understanding your own values which can steer your decisions, guide your career, and even lead to a happier life. Authenticity has become one of my core values because for most of my life, I played the role of a people-pleaser, losing my identity along the way. I've learned that maintaining a facade leads nowhere. In contrast, embracing authenticity does take you to your desired destination. I am a firm believer that we are all created to be distinct from one another, and this difference comes equipped with its own set of advantages and challenges. This is what makes the life ecosystem colourful in every way. When we attempt to alter our natural characteristics or fail to accept our uniqueness, we risk missing out on discovering the full potential that accompanies our creation. Authenticity begins with self-awareness and that means understanding your values, purpose, vision, strengths and weaknesses. Authenticity propels us to recognise and value our individual traits so we can build a foundation to lead a fulfilling life. This acceptance not only fosters personal growth but also contributes to a more diverse and vibrant society.

SHINE LIKE A DIAMOND

Like diamonds forged under intense pressure and extreme heat, authentic self-discovery is a profound journey deep within. Diamonds crystallise in the Earth's mantle, far below the surface, under conditions of remarkable pressure and temperature. This process, spanning millions or even billions of years, mirrors our own path to self-knowledge and authenticity. Just as diamonds require time and specific conditions to form, we too need time and experience to truly understand ourselves and discover our potential. And I have come to know that endurance and authenticity play crucial roles in this process of self-discovery. We, much like diamonds, are shaped and tested by the trials we endure in life. It is through the heat of our challenges that we emerge stronger and more brilliant. Persevering through these difficult times not only refines our character but also unveils the diamond of our true self. And what should accompany authenticity and endurance to help us discover ourselves is self-belief, gratitude and habits formation.

Self-belief drives us forward, even when the path is unclear. Gratitude shifts our focus from our shortcomings to our strengths, making our journey feel lighter and more positive. Consistently practising good habits, like setting clear goals and maintaining health, lays a strong foundation for resilience. Together, these elements not only help us manage difficulties but also enable us to thrive, turning obstacles into opportunities for growth and personal achievement. This is how we develop the resilience and brilliance of a diamond, shining through adversity with unmatched strength. This is also how we elevate our consciousness.

Your resilience is your greatest weapon; use it to push through adversity and emerge stronger, wiser and triumphant.

Endurance Beyond the Stripes of Challenges powerfully illustrates human resilience and the pursuit of self-discovery. As you face each hurdle, remember that these challenges are not just obstacles, but opportunities to reveal and refine your true strengths and character. With determination and heartfelt intention, you possess the keys to unlock unshakable triumph. Embrace the trials, for they mould you into a more authentic and liberated self, equipped to shine brightly against any adversity. Stand firm in the face of difficulty, knowing that each step forward enriches your character, empowering you to emerge not only whole but also enlightened and invigorated to continue your path to personal greatness.

Let your roar be heard and show the world your true strength with fierce elegance.

ABOUT KABINGA

'If you admit it, you can change; if you confront it, you can heal.'
– Kabinga

Kabinga C Mazaba is a rising literary talent and a dedicated mental health expert specialising in trauma recovery. Her journey, marked by overcoming childhood trauma, epitomises the extraordinary strength of the human spirit. Kabinga never thought she would become a writer and author. After being told that she was neither smart nor good enough. Writing has become her way of expressing her thoughts and has greatly helped her heal from her childhood trauma.

As a transformation and mindset coach, international speaker, keynote speaker and award-winning author of Amazon's number-one bestseller book *C.O.N.F.R.O.N.T: Reclaim Your Life,* is a guiding light for those on their paths to healing and transformation.

With deep insights into the human psyche, Kabinga creates a nurturing space for self-realisation amidst life's complexities. Her coaching helps clients navigate their mental landscapes, moving from self-doubt to clarity and authentic self-awareness. Onstage, Kabinga captivates audiences with her magnetic presence, sharing stories of resilience that inspire and act as catalysts for personal change. Her blend of compassion and strength positions her as a bridge-builder, guiding people from their past selves to their full potential.

In her relentless pursuit of knowledge, Kabinga is actively working towards a degree in counselling, underscoring her deep commitment to aiding individuals in overcoming challenges, finding peace after trauma, and embarking on journeys of profound personal growth. She hosts the podcast, *The Uncomfortable Stuff*, which breaks the silence on life's challenges, encouraging listeners to unpack their burdens and embrace life with purpose and peace.

Kabinga's philosophy, 'Life is a journey, embrace uncertainty,' reflects her belief in the power of resilience and adaptability. This principle infuses her personal and professional endeavours with purpose and determination, guiding her in making impactful contributions to the mental health field.

Balancing her professional achievements, Kabinga is a nurturing mother of three and a loving wife, exemplifying her belief in harmonising career aspirations with family life. Her story is not just about personal triumph but also about empowering others through empathy and compassion. Her WHY for her career extends beyond her narrative, fuelled by an unwavering desire to support others in their healing, ensuring everyone can find happiness and live authentically.

Her book *C.O.N.F.R.O.N.T: Reclaim Your Life* is more than a memoir of Kabinga's journey through trauma; it's a testament to human resilience. Through sharing her experiences, she aims to offer hope and inspiration to those lost in the shadows, providing the courage needed to confront their challenges and reclaim their lives. Kabinga C Mazaba is a role model for personal growth, symbolising the potential to rise from adversity and inspire a world needing hope and understanding. With Kabinga, inspiration isn't just a word; it's an experience that will elevate you towards your envisioned life.

HEAR US ROAR: TIGER EDITION

Website: kabingamazaba.com (Coming soon)
Facebook: facebook.com/kabingamazaba
Instagram: instagram.com/kabingamazaba
LinkedIn: linkedin.com/in/kabingamazaba

KAREN WEAVER
FINDING PURPOSE

There are many times in life where I have had to tap into my passion and purpose. It has to be part of my DNA because it's what keeps us alive and motivated; feeling like life is an adventure. Whenever we are passionate about something, we're enthusiastic, we connect in with it. It feels new and fresh and energised. Our passion is what we need to keep our burning desire alive. And when we align it with our values and our purpose, it becomes *our calling;* it is what we are called to, our divine duty on this Earth. It's not a head thing, it's a heart thing. If I had used my head and had thought into it, I would never have believed that the power of story was where my destiny would lie.

Yes, my mother read a lot. She loved reading books and still does … I cannot even imagine how many books my mother has read in her lifetime, so that's her thing. Whereas mine is the power of story, and it stemmed from me realising my burning desire for *story*.

The teachable moments that can happen through story are so powerful. Whether it be fiction or non-fiction, it doesn't matter, because whenever your story reaches the heart and mind of the person it is destined to reach, you change their life in that moment. It can heal them, ignite a passion or a burning desire within them, or educate them. If you show up for story, which is my absolute passion in life, amazing things happen.

Words are powerful and when used for 'good' they have a ripple effect around the world. I believe stories are what makes the world go round. I identified that in my childhood, Growing up in Ireland, as a *parky*, in a two bedroom home, with four kids, as well as mum and dad, it was so interesting. But it was being a parky that really helped me see, as in reflection, it really helped me see that sense of community. A *parky* was what we called everyone who lived 'on the park'; everyone in our little cul-de-sac, was like family. If you needed to go over to their house for sugar or anything, really, that's what you did.

Whenever something happened, or someone would visit, or a child had a dream, then someone in the *park* would know somebody, or have someone related to them, who would come and have a cup of tea and share their stories around their experience. That was *gold*. It was like a mentorship. But it was just something that happened in Irish communities; everybody wants to help one another and support each other with their dreams. I guess, everyone wanted to help each other to *get out of the park*. But in a sense, being in the park was a beautiful thing. It's a beautiful foundation to propel from.

When I was nine, we moved out of the park and my dad built his dream home on a hill. Now, for *a parky* to do that was phenomenal. But it was my first experience of watching manifestation in motion, seeing my dad achieve his dream. I remember us going to look at the empty field, and he couldn't afford the whole field, so we bought half the field, and he bought the highest part of the field.

We lived in a park beside the Catholic Church. It was pretty significant when we moved, because we were moving a mile and a half up the road, but it was moving from the south of Ireland to the north of Ireland. At the top of the hill, we looked out and could see the two steeples of the Protestant Church and the Catholic Church in the town where we lived. Moving out of the park, meant our lives were going to change … a lot. But being a parky has been at my core. And stories were always a big part of that. Not just gossip, but actual stories that helped to advance people. People would stick up for each other, and support each other and teach the value of true stories. It was just such a powerful foundation

So I've always had *the parky* in me, and it is that power of story that was so passionate about the community. Back then, there were no telephones. You went to the phone at the end of the street if you wanted to call someone. It was wonderful; everyone looked out for each other and If somebody died, everyone would rally around to support and hold and have space for that person.

That has led to one of my passions; holding space for story, to go out and reach the hearts and minds of the people who need it, because that's how we have a ripple effect in a world that's broken. That's how we heal it, just like Kintsugi. In Japan when a vase is broken, that doesn't mean it's unfixable. If it's put back together with the golden thread of love, and will be more beautiful than it ever was before. Yes, a little fragile, but beautiful. And that's okay. And that is why I'm so passionate about story, because stories share a vulnerable side.

Words can connect, change things and change people … and change starts within us all. My purpose in life is to help awaken those who sleep to their potential. We can do that by igniting something deep within them, a burning desire, waking them to their potential that anything is possible in life. And that is my purpose on this Earth. I will do that through story. I will do that through books. I will do it through videos. I will do it by connecting with people through events.

It's all fuelled by story. Every one of us is a living story. We are all writing new chapters every single day of our lives. Whenever a chapter ends, it's time to write a new one. A transition happens. We need stories more than ever then, because we need the support and guidance through the transition, and we have to work on ourselves. If we don't do the self-development needed, then we are left behind or we don't transition to our highest ability. During that struggle, we retreat and go backwards and keep rewriting the same chapter again and again, where instead we're supposed to end that chapter and move on to the next chapter of our life, to live life to its fullest. That's where the magic is. It takes courage. But if you can endure the struggle, do the work and plant the seeds, that's when you are ready. When divine timing and circumstance align, that's when the magic happens, the breakthrough happens, and we get to write our next chapter. But you need to stick the course. You need to have faith. You need to do all of the wonderful things.

I loved learning Napoleon Hill's principles though his book, *Think and Grow Rich*. It's a book that everyone should read. Well, more than read, everyone should study. Each of those thirteen principles will gift you something whenever you feel into them. Your sixth sense, faith, persistence, all of those things. The mastermind is knowing we're never alone. We can call in all of the support and guidance we need, but we must learn to ask. This journey is led by us. We have to go inwards, do the work, and lean outwards for the support to make it happen. And that happens through books like *Think and Grow Rich*.

The book by Harry R. Moody and David M. Carroll called *'The Five Stages of the Soul*, is where I learned a lot about the struggle and the breakthrough. It's in stages three and four where people get stuck. That's where they retreat and go into fear. That's where people lose belief in themselves because they're being tested. But if you endure the test, you never have to do that test again. Breakthrough will happen. Learn the lessons. Listen. Be guided.

Another thing I'm so passionate about right now is how self-discipline is self-love. It's about showing up for myself first, so I can be the best version of myself for others. It's so important, especially for me as a mum of six. to show up and be *that* every day. I have to continuously make sure I'm pouring into myself, otherwise, I'll have nothing left to give to others. I've been there before. When I didn't practise self-love, I fell into PTSD. I wasn't up in high vibrational thoughts and frequencies. And so, when something challenging happened in life, as happens to us all, I struggled. Normally, I wouldn't have, it would have just been a bump, but because I was tinkering on the line, I fell and I sunk to the bottom.

But I endured that.

And when I awakened, I went through an awakening to my potential, and to what's possible in life. I awakened to the important things and found the passion to help others, and help myself, to maintain a vibration and frequency at a high-level to ensure good things came into our life.

That's when my life started to change. We're all going to go through ebbs and flows and transitions. We're always going to be reaching higher and moving upwards. That's what we're supposed to do. That is what we're here to do. We're not meant to be stagnant. Change is inevitable. It's constant. And so my passion and purpose is to make life an adventure. And with the fuel of passion, the burning desire, and with the absolute armour that is living in purpose, I know that I will have the skills and tools I need to live a fulfilled life … because I'm fearless and I have faith and I am doing the work. Now, whenever life happens, I don't fall below the line. I have the tools I need to stay up there. I stumble a bit, dust myself off, get myself realigned and declutter all that no longer serves me. When my daughter was very ill, … it felt like it was happening *to me*, but it wasn't. I was there in a supporting role for that chapter in her life. It's important to remember that.

And finally, remember that being passionate and purposeful is a commitment to life. Because when we have a burning desire and keep it in front of us and align that with our purpose and our values, then we are moving forward with a zest for life. Then when all of our actions can align with that, and we will never live in regret.

When we awaken to our passion and purpose, life shifts from surviving to thriving. We begin to see that every story - ours included - is a living testament to what's possible when we align our hearts with our calling.

I'm here, not just as an author, a publisher and mother of six, but as a woman who has walked through fire and chosen to rise, again and again, with my heart wide open. My path has been messy and magnificent, and what I've learned is this - your passion is your compass, and your purpose is your anchor. Together, they will guide you home to your true self.

So, don't hold back. Let your story out. Let it echo into the hearts of those who are waiting for your words, your voice, your truth. This is how we heal the world—one awakened soul at a time.

TAKEAWAY TIPS TO ALIGN WITH YOUR PASSION & PURPOSE

1. *Start with Your Story:* Reflect on where you've come from - your struggles, your joys, your turning points. There is gold in your story, and often your purpose is hidden in the pages you've already lived.
2. *Follow What Sparks You:* What is that thing that lights you up? That's your passion talking. Don't dismiss it. Lean into what energises and excites you. That spark is your soul saying, "This way."
3. *Align Your Actions with Your Values:* Purpose isn't about what looks good on paper, it's about what feels true. Make sure your daily choices match your inner truth, not external expectations.
4. *Commit to Inner Work:* Your outer purpose can't shine without inner alignment. Meditate. Journal. Read. Heal. Do what it takes to stay in tune with your higher self. Self-discipline is self-love.
5. *Surround Yourself with Soulful Support*: You're not meant to do this alone. Call in your mastermind, your tribe, your mentors. Be around those who fan your flame, not dampen your light.

So here's to you writing new chapters, rising into your calling, and choosing to live a passionate, purposeful life with courage, conviction, and soul. Keep going. The world needs your light.

ABOUT KAREN

Karen is an award-winning publisher, author, TEDx Speaker and advanced law of attraction practitioner.

Author of numerous books across many genres – fiction, motivational, children's and journals – she chooses to lead the way in her authorship generously sharing her philosophies through her writing.

Karen is also a sought-after speaker who shares her knowledge and wisdom on building publishing empires, establishing yourself as a successful author-publisher and book writing.

Having built a highly successful publishing business from scratch, signing major authors, writing over forty books herself and establishing her own credible brand in the market, Karen has developed strategies and techniques based on tapping into the power of knowing to create your dreams.

Karen is a gifted teacher who inspires others to make magic happen in their lives through her seven life principles that have been integral in her success.

When time and circumstance align, magic happens.

Website: kpwofficial.com

LAURA MUIRHEAD
A RECIPE FOR SUCCESS

Have you ever considered how people are able to accomplish their dreams? These days, this is frequently referred to as *manifesting*. You might even roll your eyes at the word or the idea of *manifesting* because it's used so much lately. But, have you considered how people are actually able to reach their goals, build a business, manifest their dreams?

I can only speak from my experience. And, throughout my life, I've had many times where I've been able to attain my goal, or create a business (more than one) and fulfill my dreams.

It starts as a thought, an idea, a creative spark if you will. You see, something or an idea, a thought comes to you. It might not get planted at first, maybe you let the thought pass the first time, but somehow, the thought keeps coming back to you … you just can't let it go. The idea is formed and is living in your brain and you just can't shake it. It then starts to move into your heart. This is where the passion starts to grow.

Let me give you an example. When I was about eleven years old, I got a new bike. It was time for a bigger bike than what I had, and I even spent some of my birthday money on it. I was happy with my bike, it was nice. I remember it being white. It was a great bike for me. It wasn't long after that I saw another bike. This other bike was … well … it was really cool. I couldn't shake the idea of this other bike. The seed had been planted. But, honestly, I had a perfectly good, new bike already. I didn't *need* another bike. And what would my parents say anyway? I had no use for two bikes. Was I just being ungrateful for what I had?

Still, I kept thinking about the cool bike. At some point a thought and idea came to me. I had a cousin who was about a year older than me. What if I bought the cool bike and gave my cousin my current bike? I still had some birthday money. I could buy the bike on my own. This was something that might work. It gave my idea a purpose. Maybe my parents would even go for that plan. I somehow had to find the courage to ask my parents to ok my plan. Well, they did.

Seeing my cousin with his new bike was well worth it. Watching him as he happily decorated his new bike with decals to make it his own was a bonus for me that I hadn't thought of. It really was a winning plan for both of us.

A couple of years later, I heard my grandparents planning a trip to Finland. My grandpa had grown up in Finland, after being born in the States. Grandma's parents had migrated from Finland, so they both had relatives there to visit. It was a big trip for them. Letters were written to relatives to work out the details. Remember, this was well before the internet, and even a phone call overseas was limited because of the cost.

I had an idea that maybe I could go with them to Finland. The seed was planted in me and began to grow. It moved into my heart. The desire was real! Just like with the bike, at some point I needed the courage to ask both my parents and my grandparents this time.

I had to form a plan. It was to save my money. By then, I was old enough to earn money by babysitting. I was also fortunate to have a great aunt who generously gave money for birthdays and Christmas, not only to me, but to all of her family. I felt that I could be diligent and save all my money to put towards my trip. After all, I had some time before we were going to travel.

Here's where things get good. Once you have your idea, and it has grown into a passion, AND you have a plan with action that you are taking, things happen that you might not expect. The universe will conspire with you. In this case, it was in the form of my generous great aunt. When she heard about my dream and plan for Finland, she said she wanted to give me extra money here and there, to help me save for my trip.

How amazing was that?

I did save my money, and in the summer of 1976, I went with my grandparents to visit our relatives in Finland. It was my first trip and their last trip there. When I planned and took that trip, I had no idea that in the future I would connect with more relatives who would visit me in the US, but I would also have more trips to Finland with my son.

As I mentioned, in my life, this has played out many times. Oftentimes my ideas have been formed out of frustration or uncomfortable circumstances.

If you've read my memoir, *A Funny Thing Happened on the Way to My Life,* you'll remember that I didn't love the situation I was growing up in. By the time I was in high school, I knew I had to find a way to get out of the house.

It came to my awareness that graduating early from school was an option. It was somewhat common to graduate a semester early. A less common, but available option, was to graduate a full year early. This is what I wanted to explore. I researched the requirements and put my plan into action. It worked and I graduated from high school in three years.

As it turned out, the summer I graduated created more discomfort in my living arrangements at home, and I ended up moving out to live with my best friend's family, eventually moving to California with them.

Over the years, my thoughts, passions and plans have led me to achieve a private pilot's license, multiple businesses, and even finding and reconnecting with someone I met over thirty years ago, now my husband.

I have built a horse stable from a cornfield up. That was born from another uncomfortable situation and a desire to fill the gap with something that would work better, at least in my mind, than the available options.

My horses were boarded at a stable close to my house. After my son was bitten by the owner's dog and she didn't comply with keeping the dog contained, I knew I had to move to another stable. The only option was a stable about twenty minutes away. So, I moved one horse there and my show horse was moved to my trainer's stable, forty-five minutes away. It was a decent plan. As it turned out, my first horse had a disease that required medicine twice a day. The owner of the stable said she would give him the meds, but I discovered she wasn't always on top of that. I tried my best to try to fill in the gaps and get to the stable to give him his medicine at the right times, but as you might imagine, with two young children, it wasn't always easy. I was frustrated for sure and wanted a better, more convenient situation.

I started to look around for a stable to buy, even making an offer to the stable owner whose dog bit my son. That didn't work out. Someone I knew mentioned her friend was selling some land in the town where I lived. Well, there was something I hadn't thought of originally. The rest, as they say, is history. I built a stable on that land and created a business offering riding lessons and horse boarding. There was a purpose to my desire. Yes, it served me, but it also served many others.

Being in an uncomfortable place also was the creative spark for me to have my own pottery and art studio. I was learning to throw clay at a local art centre. I loved it and I loved working with my mentor. Turns out I had a talent for it as well.

To this day, I don't understand why, but there were a few people at the art centre who behaved poorly. At one point, a ceramic piece I had created 'disappeared' right out of the kiln … for a whole year. I'm surprised it was even found then. The whole place had been searched when my bowl originally went missing, and when it was discovered, it was in a place that had definitely been searched. There was also verbal abuse directed at me.

Initially, I didn't think about creating my own workspace. I just knew I couldn't continue to create in that environment. Then a thought was born. A seed was planted.

Once that took root my passion grew. I considered different options, eventually deciding to buy a building with a creative workspace, as well as retail space to sell my creations … my pottery, photography and artwork.

After enjoying that experience for five years, I recently made the decision it was time to move on and I closed the studio. Even that has opened up opportunities for my next passions to unfold.

My first business grew out of an opportunity I couldn't let go of. My friends lived near a bread store that became quite popular in their town. What if we were able to franchise that store? It seemed like a good fit for all of us to go into business together, each of us bringing different skills to the table.

Again, the seed had been planted. My thoughts became a desire, a plan was formed and action was taken. There was a lot to learn but we did it. We opened the store. However, we were naive and ignorant to many things. We hired what we thought was a competent lawyer to negotiate the lease and give us advice. We all did what we could, but the business failed. It was only later we discovered that the owner of the original store hadn't been truthful about his financial situation.

Even though we had the best of intentions and fulfilled our desire, it hadn't been built on a solid foundation. Lessons were learned that have served me in other projects.

One thing I have learned, is that your mindset, your attitude and showing gratitude are huge game changers.

Last year, I set a revenue goal for our family business. Initially, I didn't tell my business partner, my husband, what my goal for the year was. I anchored it in by using it for login passwords. My intention was set. I knew we could reach that goal. Once I shared my number for the year with my husband, he wasn't as confident. I didn't let his doubts come into play. I know how energy works and I stayed in a higher vibration about this goal.

You probably won't be surprised when I tell you that we did reach that income for the year in our business. Of course we are thrilled! The momentum of that is carrying over to this year for our company and we are off to a great start, with a fresh seed planted for what we can achieve. Let's not forget that we have a purpose with our company goals. A passion and purpose to deliver the best service to our customers, but also to support our employees in the best ways we can. We reach out to local vocational schools to bring in fresh graduates giving them employment opportunities. Additionally, we offer training programs for all employees to expand their skills and knowledge.

That is the ripple effect. It's not just success for us, it's also for our employees and their families. We don't take any of this for granted and are immensely grateful. We also have an intention to give back by donating to charities. Whether you support local or globally, you may never see your personal ripple but know that it's happening.

This is what I want you take with you:

Start out with a thought. It might even be a passing thought at first, but then there are signs that keep bringing your attention back to that thought, that idea. You just know that there is something there. Something you just have to do. Your desire, your passion for it grows and is real. You start to realise that you are forming a plan. There are actions that you can take. And once that happens, once you start to take action, it seems like things start to fall into place. This is where the universe meets you. Even though you have a plan in place, once everything is in motion, it's important to allow for the unexpected. Yes, have a plan, but don't hold so tightly to it that you miss opportunities that you didn't realise could play out. Let go of the 'how' and be open to the magic that can happen.

I recently read a quote: 'Do your worrying before you place your bet, not after the wheel starts turning.' I love this analogy to let go of the 'how' once you've put your wheels in motion.

An important part in all of this is, from the beginning, imagine how you will *feel* as you move through your actions, but especially once you've achieved your desire, your goal. What does that feel like? Are you excited, proud, happy?

And keep your purpose in mind as well. Your purpose is what will continue to fuel your passion. It continues to give your desire the energy to move forward. Once you have succeeded to fill your passion with the best intentions and purpose, you will also realise that this will have a ripple effect, touching people in ways you hadn't thought of.

I learned from the best, my great aunt who was so generous in helping me fulfill my dream of travelling to Finland, and from many other personal goals I've had over the years, that there is great purpose in giving to others. This can also be a strong passion.

I have found that allowing your own thoughts and ideas to be planted as seeds of passions, then following your passion and partnering that passion with purpose and a plan, leaving room for magic, is a recipe for success in your life.

So, are you looking for the recipe for success in your life?

Start by allowing the seeds of your thoughts and ideas to be planted.

Add a drop of passion and partner it with purpose.

Create a plan and start to take action.

And the final ingredient? Leave room for magic.

ABOUT LAURA

Laura Muirhead is an internationally acclaimed author, accomplished artist and the CFO of her family's multimillion-dollar company. She is also the creator of the Queen Code program and the Queen Code Oracle Card Deck, which guide multipassionate women to find clarity, set boundaries and elevate both life and business, stepping into their full potential. Laura's work bridges creativity and business, demonstrating that success can be achieved on both sides of the spectrum.

Her personal journey is as dynamic as her professional life – she is a licensed pilot, an energy healer, and the author of *A Funny Thing Happened on the Way to My Life*, as well as a beloved children's book and three journals. Laura's life story is one of resilience and reinvention. From navigating the unexpected twists of life to rebuilding after a devastating house fire, she draws inspiration from her experiences to empower others.

Laura enjoys photography and exploring the world. She splits her time between homes in New Jersey and Michigan. Laura cherishes time with her husband, grown children, close friends, two Labrador retrievers, and a life filled with creativity and adventure. Learn more about Laura by visiting afunnythinghappenedonthewaytomylife.com.

LOUISE LALLY
THE POWER OF BORROWED BELIEF

THE EARLY STRUGGLES: A SINGLE PARENT'S JOURNEY

When I look back at my life, I often think of the times when I didn't believe in myself. I was a single parent, juggling the daily challenges of raising my child while trying to build a career.

There were many nights I stayed up late, wondering if I was doing enough, if I was good enough. The weight of responsibility was heavy, and there were moments when I doubted my ability to balance it all.

Being a single parent often made me feel isolated. It wasn't just the physical load of looking after my child, it was the emotional toll, the constant questioning of whether I was capable of being everything I needed to be. *Was I a good mother? Was I capable of giving my child the future I wanted for him? Could I build a career at the same time?*

For so long, I found it difficult to trust myself. My self-doubt crept into every aspect of my life. I would wonder if I was cut out for more - if I had the talent or the capacity to do something greater with my life, something that went beyond the routine of getting by. But despite those feelings of uncertainty, something kept me moving forward. It wasn't always obvious, but there was a small voice deep inside that refused to give up. It was the belief that, somehow, there was more ahead of me, though I didn't know exactly how to find it yet.

DISCOVERING THE POWER OF BORROWED BELIEF

I spent over sixteen years working in retail. At first, it was just a way to earn a living and provide for my family, but as time passed, I found myself climbing the ranks, taking on more responsibilities, and eventually stepping into leadership roles. It was during these years that I started to see something important about myself, something I had been blind to for so long.

It wasn't always my own belief in myself that carried me through difficult times, it was the belief of others. I started to realise that there were people around me who saw something in me that I couldn't see. I remember several key moments where a mentor, a colleague, or even a manager would say, 'I believe in you,' and it was that belief, that confidence in me from others, that helped me take the next step forward.

At first, I didn't understand the significance of this. I thought it was just kindness or support. But over time, I saw how those moments of encouragement could spark something inside me – something I didn't even know I had. When others believed in me, I found it easier to believe in myself, even if it was just a little bit more each day.

I call this *borrowed belief*, because it was the belief of others that I borrowed to move forward. I didn't have that belief in myself at first, but through the kindness and encouragement of others, I began to discover it.

THE STRUGGLE WITH SELF-DOUBT AND THE TURNING POINT

Despite these experiences, I still struggled with self-doubt. There were times when the thought of stepping into a leadership role, speaking in front of an audience, or taking a risk terrified me. I would question whether I was truly capable of succeeding in anything beyond what I had already achieved.

But something shifted in me. After years of working hard and proving myself in various roles, I finally had the courage to face my fears. And in doing so, I realised that what I had been lacking all along, was a deeper belief in my own worth. I had always waited for others to tell me I was good enough before I could believe it myself.

This was the turning point. I realised that I didn't need to wait for someone else's approval or encouragement. I had already borrowed enough belief from others to build my own. And in that moment, everything changed. I finally understood that self-belief wasn't something that just appeared overnight, it was something I had to work on, something I had to nurture.

THE TEDX TALK: WHERE BORROWED BELIEF CAME FULL CIRCLE

My TEDx talk, *The Power of Borrowed Belief,* came at a time when I had finally started to see how far I'd come. I reflected on my journey as a single mother, my struggles with self-doubt, and the people who had helped me believe in myself along the way. It was during this talk that I truly understood the power of external belief, and how it can fuel someone who is unsure of their own potential.

Standing on the TEDx stage in Galway in Ireland, I spoke not just about my professional experiences, but about my personal journey; how the belief of others shaped who I became. I shared the stories of the people who had believed in me when I couldn't believe in myself and how I had also believed in others without realising the enormous impact it had. That was when I knew this was where my true purpose lay: helping others see their own potential, even when they couldn't see it for themselves.

It was humbling to share my story, to stand in front of an audience and tell them that the belief of others had been the catalyst for my own self-belief. And in sharing that, I was able to inspire others to believe in themselves too. That talk was not just the culmination of my journey, it was a celebration of everything I had overcome and all the people who had lifted me up along the way.

THE LEGACY OF BORROWED BELIEF

Today, I look back on everything I've achieved, and see how far I've come. The road wasn't easy. There were many nights when I questioned my worth, my ability and my future, but through it all, there were people who saw something in me and believed in me. It was this borrowed belief that carried me forward, step by step.

What I've learned is this: self-belief is not something that magically appears on its own; it's built over time, with support, encouragement, and sometimes a little bit of borrowed belief. And it's this belief, whether it's our own or someone else's, that can propel us forward, even when the road ahead feels uncertain.

I've realised that my journey is just beginning. Every day, I continue to learn, grow, and challenge myself, but I carry with me the understanding that belief in oneself, or borrowed belief, is what makes the impossible possible.

ABOUT LOUISE

Louise Lally is an award-winning business coach, leadership trainer, and the founder of the Louise Lally Training Academy, based in Galway, Ireland. With over fifteen years of experience in the retail and service sectors, Louise has become a leading voice in customer experience strategy, people development, and organisational leadership.

Through her academy, Louise offers a broad suite of services including leadership development, one-to-one business coaching, customer experience design and team performance training. She has worked with a diverse range of clients across Ireland, from independent entrepreneurs to large-scale retail and service organisations. Her work is grounded in the belief that when people are empowered and supported, businesses thrive.

Louise's approach is people-centered, practical and transformational. Drawing from her extensive background in operations and team leadership, she designs programs that not only enhance business performance but also cultivate confident, emotionally intelligent leaders. Her signature programs focus on personal leadership, emotional resilience and creating positive, high-performing workplace cultures.

As a certified coach with qualifications in executive coaching, neuro-linguistic programming (NLP) and emotional intelligence, Louise brings both depth and versatility to her practice. Her coaching style is empathetic yet results-driven, and she is known for her ability to unlock clarity, purpose and motivation in those she works with. Her clients consistently praise her for her insight, professionalism and unwavering belief in their potential.

Beyond her coaching and training work, Louise is a sought-after speaker and contributor on topics such as leadership, business growth, mindset and customer experience. She is regularly invited to speak at events, facilitate workshops and contribute to industry panels. She is also deeply committed to supporting women in business, with a particular focus on empowering women to step into leadership roles with authenticity and Confidence.

Originally from Galway, Louise is proud of her roots in the West of Ireland and brings a unique blend of warmth, authenticity, and strategic thinking to her work. Her deep connection to community and passion for supporting Irish business are central to her mission at the Louise Lally Training Academy.

In all aspects of her work, Louise champions a simple but powerful philosophy from her Tedx Talk: *The Power of Borrowed Belief* Louise believes that through believing in others at times when you don't believe in yourself is something many of us can do to achieve our dreams. Through her academy, she continues to inspire business owners, leaders, and teams to take ownership of their development, lead with purpose and deliver exceptional results. Her impact is evident in the transformations she facilitates and the lasting relationships she builds with her clients.

Louise Lally is not only a coach and trainer – she is a catalyst for change, a mentor to many and a steadfast advocate for the power of people-driven success

MARAIKA MASON
EARLY LIFE CHANGES

I'm at the beginning of the latter part of my life – that is if I live to be about one hundred. Then when I get there, I can say, *I am at the other end of the beginning of the end of my life.* In hindsight, the years have flown past. Yet at times, they seemed to drag. There are so many changes to the world I knew or remembered from my early childhood. It has not been a dramatic life, nor a chaotic life, but we all face challenges as we go along life's path. It's the way we deal with the challenges and recover our peace of body and mind that define us.

Remarkably, on looking back, I have survived what I now recall as many mental hiccups, as well as physical, along the way to today. It is only in being remarked upon or discussed in conversations that I look back and wonder how so much has happened in such a short time, like my eighty-plus years. I was a child of the war years – WWII, I mean. My parents never really discussed it with me or my sisters at any time in our life and, of course, there were *secrets* never discussed.

Life was hard for my parents then, but they still fell in love, married and had children. No matter how hard it may seem, life can survive with love and connection. Whether I can recall the devastation that occurred during the war years is a moot point, as it may have been observed by my childish eyes as the strangeness of daily life. I now believe we were very lucky, as the house we lived was untouched by the bombing and still stands today. On one side, the whole house was destroyed and so were many others in the immediate area.

I was born in the house, as was one of my sisters. It was quite a common practise to have home births with just a nurse or midwife attending. I remember having to stand outside my parent's bedroom door while my sister was being born, but I did not know the reason why I was banned from entering the room, nor was it ever explained to me. Suddenly, I had another sister. My middle sister was born in a small town where my parents escaped to be safe during the pregnancy. As all lights were forbidden and there was no transport available, my father put my mother onto the back of a pushbike when it was time to take her to the small hospital. This was during a fierce snowstorm. *Can you imagine?* Some hours after my sister was born, my mother was handed the baby to feed, but something didn't feel right to her, as her baby was only a few hours old and the baby handed to her was feeding well, as if the baby was at least a couple of days old. She was assured this was her baby, but as there were no lights allowed, mistakes could happen, which was made clear to everyone when baby's nappy was changed. Yes, it was a boy!!

When we were younger and my sister got a bit tiresome as, sigh, some sisters can get, we would often ask our mother why she had to swap. *I always wanted a brother*. At this time too, we had Katya hiding in our attic. And as we had been searched before, the soldiers came back and searched for anyone we may have been hiding. We were very grateful to have received warning, so our refugee was able to hide herself inside the mattress. What a courageous woman she was; as they searched for her, they stabbed their bayonets into the mattress but she never cried out, despite many cuts. I wish I had asked my parents many more questions and written down any answers, which they were, albeit reluctantly, willing to give me.

After moving to another area, as the current one was a rental above a cafe with its nightly raucous singing and merry-making, my mother set up a small business making hand-sewn material lampshades, which our father would deliver to customers, again on his trusty bike with myself sitting on a very uncomfortable little metal seat on the back wheel – and holding on to the lampshade for dear life.

Moving forward with a positive mindset, a big decision was made to migrate to find work for both our parents and a better lifestyle for myself and my sisters. Applications were handed in. Then, there was the thorough process of seeing if we were all of sound body and mind. The *all clear* was obtained, eventually, and the proper officials were to be assured that our family would be of good upstanding and healthy citizens of our new country. Our chosen transport (although I doubt we were offered any other choice) was the migrant ship, *The Fairsea*. In our eyes, it was a HUGE ship; a converted troop ship with no cabins, just large open spaces filled with three-tier bunk beds. There were twelve bunks attached to each other, with just a small curtain at each head end for some privacy, but bunks so low you could not sit up in the beds. Adults were segregated. Men went to one end of the ship, while women and children to another. The toilet and shower facility available to each section did not offer any privacy and with two small washing basins for all to use, this led to many arguments and numerous lists made about who got to use them for washing clothes, on what day and time. This led to many fights, including hair-pulling and yelling, even slaps that occurred among women who not only needed to use the basins for their ablutions but also to keep their family clean. Everywhere we went, there was the awful reek of bleach. People threw up because of their breath catching the smell, not just the swell. Seasickness was rife for a great deal of the trip, for adults and children alike! And there were several mealtimes when I was the only one in my family sitting at our table, by myself – at aged ten.

We are still so grateful, and thankful, for the decision made by our parents for our family's future, and in making the right country choice. Although several countries made the short list and were considered. To be able to migrate, we needed a sponsor. As our chosen and willing sponsor, an uncle, had a business north-east Australia, we would have to adapt to living in a tropical city. However, the process to be approved took so long, our sponsor uncle had sold up and moved west to an outback town to run the small general store. What a contrast! We arrived to a dusty and dry town; bare earth with not a blade of grass or a leaf of anything green. We not only had to learn new ways of daily living but also learn a new language. Having no knowledge of the English language led to me sitting in a dentist chair, soon after our arrival in our new home. 'What is a dentist?' I had asked, only to be reassured, that it was, 'For your own good.' Again, in a language I did not understand, I ended up having a tooth extracted without knowing the why and what. During this time, my sisters and I were able to stay in a convent until our parents arrived. As it was school holidays, we were the only children in residence in the large, mostly empty convent. It was a scary experience, and I'm still sure we *really did* see the headless ghost wearing a Nun's habit.

Mindful is what I remember being told my parents had to be, in the small, rattly and very old rusty truck that came to pick them up from the Airport and take us to the outback Banana Plantation where we had been found a place to live *for a while*. 'Mind where you put your feet, mind to hold on tight, and mind you don't look down,' the driver told them, as the truck had very few floorboards in and he told us that looking down might make us *seasick* to see the road rushing past underneath for the next *600+km*. The driver, Tucker was his name, a true-blue Aussie bloke, said his truck may be old but he did not want anyone to throw up in it, as he would have to clean it. Of course, later on we learned that there in the outback water is more precious than gold.

The difference from busy city living to living in the outback was enormous. Not only did we need to learn a new language, there were new customs to adapt to in this *G'Day Mate* country. It was hard getting used to the *outback life*; with its cockroaches, snakes, frogs, emus and kangaroos, learning that a snake is just like an eel, only different. Going up in a helicopter for some mustering, and as passengers in the old truck for some *bush bashin*, going mushrooming without knowing the safe ones to pick, and finding out that just because you live on a banana plantation, you do not need to eat bananas for breakfast, lunch and dinner. We soon worked out that thirty minutes before the sun went down was the best time to have a quick bath in a (cut in half) old rainwater tank. Prior to sunset, the water was red hot and after that it cooled down rapidly and was too cold to sit in any longer than a few minutes.

We learned never to go to the outside dunny on your own, for it could harbour creepy critters, or in strong winds, could blow over – as my father found out one very windy day. We girls, and our mother, had a great laugh about that. Not so funny were the walls of our plantation rental 'house'. (Well, you couldn't really call it a house as it was only two rooms.) At night, the walls were covered with cockroaches that scurried when you turned your torch on them, and this led to some way of entertaining ourselves. Us three girls slept together on one mattress on the floor, and I can still remember how horrified our mother was when she found mouse droppings on our pillows, later seeing, many scurrying mice. We were thankful it was mice and not rats, I guess.

Finding a rental house in the small township eventually was a great time of learning community living and giving us a freedom we had not experienced in our past. There was so much to learn. We were the only Dutch people who had migrated to the town and were treated as *being special*; almost royalty. Being invited to parties and other community events, just so that locals could ask us to speak in our Dutch language. Organisers of one such party held at the church hall asked my mother, and the rest of the family, to come and join in but to bring a plate. Our mother did think that it must be a very poor church that could not afford to provide plates for its guests. And even though crockery was not abundant in our house, after having to leave most of it behind due to ship migrant rules, the *best* plate was brought along. Just an empty plate!

Oh what a laugh it was after it was explained that 'bring a plate' meant to bring along some treat *on said plate* to share with others. Our parents worked hard at the now defunct whaling station. Or picking beans and waiting tables. As I remember it, we never went without the basics, we even thrived.

But the hot weather of the outback town got to be too much for our family who had been born and grown up in a much colder climate. The decision was made to move, once again, to find better conditions and more work choices. And so, the trek across country to another major city was once again undertaken; never to be regretted.

There were many changes for us, but as children, we put our trust in our parents and accepted that they knew what was best for us all. With our current-day technology, how many unimaginable changes have happened in such a short time that we accept, and for the most part, just go along with for the ride.

Challenges? We had a few, but then again, they helped us to grow and adapt to becoming contributing citizens of this wonderful new country. Telling our story like this, I really wish I had kept a diary and noted all the answers my parents gave to our constant questions as, of course, memory does tend to gloss over the bad times and only remember the good.

ABOUT MARAIKA

Maraika was a long-time wildlife carer, along with her husband Paul, and it has only been in the last few years that she has given up doing active wildlife rescues. Leaving this now for the younger and more active generations to continue. She is however still involved on other levels to bring understanding, care and respect for our unique Australian wildlife. Maraika has two adult sons and always thankful they choose the lovely women they did to be their partners in life. She is also a proud grandmother to two handsome grandsons.

MARIANNE ROSE
A LETTER TO MY NIECE

My Darling Harriet,

How does one write a letter these days, in the age of Tik Tok and generative AI? Perhaps this is old-fashioned, but I have vivid memories of my childhood and my excitement upon receiving a letter in the mail from my best friend. She only lived in the next leafy suburb, and there was a playful and unexpected delight found in devouring the words when you didn't know what came next, as each line revealed some hidden thought, secret or holiday plan.

Back then, childhood days were filled with long summers running under a sprinkler, chasing the Mr Whippy van and aching sunburn behind the ears. We'd ride skateboards and bikes recklessly down the bitumen road with the other kids in the street. Sometimes we'd build forts and scramble along backyard fences, peeling honeycomb from trees and trying banana passionfruit from the vine. A passion and purpose filled life was one of adventure, as the world slowly revealed itself.

As I age (somewhat gracefully I might add!), the world curiously continues to unveil its secrets, and yet what wisdom can I share about living life with passion and purpose? What indeed is my own purpose?

I struggle with this question, as I suspect many do, and dear niece, there is no answer I've found to satisfy that niggle that there is something more. Perhaps I should then rephrase, '*There is no one, right, correct answer.*'

And the simple, though elusive reason for that, is that what drives and motivates you through life changes as you grow and evolve. Perhaps I could end my letter there, lesson taught, but let me ramble in my thoughts further.

As I write this, International Women's Day has passed us once again, and I'm reminded of my commitment to the advancement of women and girls. I strongly believe that if you can give a girl an education, her life (and the life of her community) will be better for it. This is because she has the opportunity and the ability to make choices, both personal (about her body and her health) and for her future; with education she can have independence and income to carve a path for herself and her community.

Did you know that in 1902 Australian women first gained the right to vote in federal elections, following the passage of the *Commonwealth Franchise Act* 1902? This might seem like ancient history, and perhaps it is, but notably, Australia was one of the first countries to allow women the right to vote.

So, consider this instead – when your nana was working in 1972, women had just been granted a right to equal pay, raising the overall rate of women's wages by around 30%, the pill became available and the federal *Child Care Act* 1979 was passed. It was only in the year I was born, 1979, that unpaid maternity leave entitlements came in.

The progress forward has been slow. For me, I recall my frustration at being taught by the domestic matriarchs of our family how to make strudel, as my male cousin went out boating. I realised how keenly I desired *not* to be bound by the drudgery of housework, and to be educated and take the opportunities my grandmother never had. This sparked a passion and purpose to go to university, to study law and fight for justice; justice, that most naive of notions – a drive to contribute to the good in the world, whatever that might have meant.

Today, perhaps more relevantly for your mum and me, the Workplace

Gender Equality Agency notes the total renumeration average gender pay gap sits at 21.8%. This means for every $1 on average a man (like your brother) will earn, women (like you) will earn 78 cents. That's a $28,425 difference over the course of a year. *'Not fair!'* you cry. And rightly so. Hence, why we must be proud and passionate to bring about purpose-led change. Things are moving in the right direction and with every voice, a new change arises to improve conditions for the better. For example, with the amendment to the *Workplace Gender Equality Act* 2012 (Cth) employers with a workforce of one hundred or more employees are now required to publish their gender pay gap data.

Perhaps all this talk of women's rights and equality bores you at your tender age. More interesting to you might be the familial questions. Such as why you have no cousins on your dad's side. (And that is an inquisitive and natural question to ask.) For many women, motherhood is a calling, but for some it's not to be. By the time your uncle came into my life, the clock was ticking, and within the year we'd eloped against the harbourside backdrop of Sydney. This is not some teary story of IVF rounds, no, we fell pregnant fairly easily. The tears came after. Almost immediately, I was beset by *hyperemesis gravidarum,* and hospitalised and, yet being told how 'good' I looked due to the stark weight loss. And then the scans showed what I already knew; the pregnancy was unviable. After that, the kindly obstetrician clarified the reality of my situation, if I tried again, the risk was certain and untenable.

So, the passion and purpose to start a nuclear family was rendered null and void. We explored fostering and adoption, but the length of time, the cost and the heartbreak wasn't for us, and a new reality emerged, to embrace being *sans* child.

Passion and purposes then waxed and waned. I moved jobs, travelled, joined committees and boards, bought a house and became a fur-mama; which inspired by the playful antics of Hamish Gruff, led me to write the book for your brother. (Sam was so little and young, and so far away in Melbourne, that it made me smile that he'd have something from his wayward aunt through COVID lockdowns.)

I find myself frustrated. *Passion* and *purpose* are such glorious and lofty goals but can so often be bandied about. '*How To*' and cliched guides reference ways to inspire you to find that elusive calling. As if by some secret sauce, if we muse on the methodology, all will seeming be revealed in earnest epiphany. Then, I too, could solve all my life's ills with a detailed description boxed as a sixty-second elevator pitch.

But no, you and I are far more multifarious women than that. We need more than the trite idea that if we find our passion or purpose, *we'll never work a day in our lives.*

Rather, we are petulant in our curiosity. I already see it in you too; your dad told me how you'd remarked defiantly in your first week of school that you, '*haven't learnt anything yet!*'

My wish for you then, dear niece, is to live life in the exquisite embrace of incessant inquisitiveness. This humble trait has led me to volunteer with people with disabilities in England, study civil law in Florence, FIFO to Darwin and live around Australia saying *YES* to opportunity. Then, as life will, the hurts and heartbreaks, the grindstone and grit, and disarray and disorder that is thrown at us all in this world, will be where you find that humble passion and purpose.

In persistent resilience to change course, adapt and surge forward in the face of life, use inquisitiveness to salt your wounds, just as I have tried to do. It is in this act of rebellion; to defy the world as it attempts to pin you to stigma, status and station; that passion and purpose will be found.

Passions are internal, felt at your core. In passions, we're given an innate sense of joy and gratification. Purpose is external, projecting outwards to others. In purpose, we're given a direction to pursue.

I waited for *le grande epiphany*, imagining I could feel the winds of change in the air. And while I waited with curiosity, I followed that intriguing little white rabbit of interests and whims, finding passion and purpose to be transitory in nature. This means, by definition, we can be multi-passionate and voluminous in the aspirations we set for ourselves.

Fear not that there may indeed be moments in life where you have no momentum. You may struggle to find a passion or purpose to relate to, let alone motivate you. During my convalescence, my mind was eerily quiet. There was no inner voice of curiosity stimulating my senses. In these moments of grief, illness and other hardships, passion is stripped away, and with it, any purpose. At these times, it is enough to be kind to yourself. Simple acts of self-care, like walking a precious pooch or making a cup of tea in your favourite mug, are enough. Personally, I like to light a candle at dusk, the gentle aroma and simple action marks a loving shift between work and home, and a closure to the day.

In the unrelenting heat of a Perth night, I reflected that I'd tried to write you a book once. I could have had you go on pirating adventures, marauding across the high seas, swashbuckling tales of courage and heroism. While I had a purpose, the passion was lacking. Perhaps stunted and muted by a mind that wants more for you, these ideas could barely reach a simmer. Why? Why was that? Where was my inspiration and creativity? As this letter reveals, I think it lives in wanting you to have the opportunities that generations before you strived for but never quite grasped. Why, rather than a teacher or a nurse, a lawyer or a doctor, you could aspire to solve the problems of our time, creating the next generation of AI tools that improve our quality of life, negotiating international supply chain deals to improve access to water, food and clean energy, speaking diplomatic languages to negotiate peace in a conflict zone. Who knows what you will aspire to be, but I dream a world for you of something more.

So, this letter is penned for you sweet Hattie and whatever you may choose. Be multi-passionate; try as many experiences as possible, seek adventure. Purpose need not be a grand statement played on social media for all to see. It can also be as humble and unpretentious as planting a winding jasmine along your fence to grow weeping into a laneway for the neighbour's to adore. The choice is yours alone, and this way you will always find a passion and purpose that enthralls, enlightens and entertains you.

With love,
Mx.

PS. As a final footnote, I presently ponder what internal passion will spring forth from the depths of my imagination that I might explore. Where might that next inner calling take me? What purpose might it reveal to share with others? This time my purpose was brought forward by a writer's deadline (it always helps). The mechanics of my brain stoked a furnace of ideas and reignited a passion to write something for you. The goal, to share with others my musings on passion and purpose and how we might grow into ourselves. I sit under the cool air conditioning as the heatwave rolls through Perth, waiting for the afternoon breeze of the Fremantle Doctor to meander in. Sweet milky tea almost finished, and a little fur-baby patiently awaiting his evening stroll, and I pause and ponder where my musings might lead.

ABOUT MARIANNE

Marianne is a non-executive director and legal practitioner with over twenty years of experience in the energy, infrastructure and banking sectors. She serves as a trusted business advisor, helping corporations develop strategic legal and integrity-driven solutions to complex challenges.

An award-winning author, Marianne penned *Hamish McGruff: The Lightning and the Thunder Jacket* and has been recognised as a NAWIC Crystal Vision Finalist. She was also featured in the #CelebratingWomen campaign. With a strong background in women's rights advocacy, Marianne is deeply committed to mentoring in governance and ethics. She was awarded a scholarship by Women in Leadership to their esteemed Advanced Women in Leadership Program, complementing her qualifications in executive and organisational coaching.

Marianne holds a BA/LLB (Hons) from Monash University and a master's of law from Melbourne University Law School. Passionate about law, ethics and women's rights, she brings a blend of emotional intelligence, integrity and innovative thinking to her professional endeavours.

MELISSA HOMEWOOD
DIS-EASE

'If you don't make time for your wellness, you will be forced to make time for your illness.' – Joyce Sunada

I once thought my 'passion and purpose' was being a successful businesswoman, a great chef, the perfect wife, a doting mother, a loyal friend and, just in general, a good person.

I believed that getting through all that life had thrown at me constituted my success.

However, the moment I found out I had cancer, none of the accomplishments I had made in life made any sense. The journey of a breast cancer diagnosis made me question my life in a million different ways. Being forced to stop was the biggest wake-up call of my life. And I didn't listen to any of the signs. There is only so much you can bury in life, and if you do it for too long, you're going to suffer the consequences. Here I was, diagnosed with breast cancer at forty-six years of age.

'When we live in a state of dis-ease, we eventually end up creating disease.' – Sarah Dakhill

I have never really dealt with the fact I was born when my mother was still a child herself, at sixteen years old.

I have never dealt with the fact my father was absent until I met him when I was sixteen, and we have never had a close relationship. I was sexually abused at the age of six by my mum's boyfriend and told if I said anything he would kill my mum and brother. I was put into a physically and mentally abusive foster home at the age of seven, along the years being used for financial gain also, I left said foster home after being physically abused up until the age of nineteen, at that time, still having my head beaten against brick walls. I rebelled with sex and alcohol in my late teens, and had a long, dysfunctional, faithless relationship in my twenties, which was also abusive and traumatic. I constantly looked for love in all the wrong places. I was rejected by many, all the while wondering where I belonged in this life and what love truly was, never knowing who truly loved me.

Some sad circumstances one might say, however, I continued on with life, working hard to prove my worth.

Chef apprentice of the year awards, employee of the month awards, head chef by nineteen, cheffing for media and sponsors at the Sydney Olympics, all while partying my hardest to forget the real pains of life and back it up by being my best.

I feel like I got myself together when I was twenty-three. I left my dysfunctional relationship in Sydney, moved to the sunny Gold Coast, became celibate and truly started enjoying my own self.

Eighteen months later I met a guy, had some more fun and had a beautiful baby boy. I took three months off to enjoy and breastfeed him but was then straight back to work. I mean, now I look back, I think how crazy it was that I didn't take more time off to enjoy the miracle I had just carried and birthed. I was always working casually too, which resulted in me never having any holidays – note to others; *don't do that!*

With the joy of becoming a mum and some wonderful travel between states, finally settling in the Pilbara in Western Australia, and with years of trying for another miracle, I became pregnant at twenty-nine with my daughter. At that point, for me, life seemed complete. Blessed with the perfect pigeon pair and knowing what unconditional love was, my heart burst at the seams both times I became a mum. I worked up until I had my daughter (standard joke in the wet mess – I would have her on the floor!) and again, was back at work just weeks later. My husband and I have had to work very hard to provide the best we can for our children. Providing what we could never have, has been the greatest yet most exhausting pleasure of life. There has always been a looming pressure for us both, as without parents ourselves, we have had no-one else to rely on, ask for help or fall back on.

We certainly have had some extremely trying times, financially.

Gosh, we couldn't afford a deposit on our own home until we were thirty-five!

However, we have provided our best and are proud that our children have never gone without … and for that we are proud.

So here I was in my forties, grounded with a beautiful home, hubby, kids, dogs and in the most gorgeous little city in the south of WA and life seemed perfect … really. Watching the kids develop, even with their little difficulties, seemed like such a gift. When our kids were in their early teens, I took on a cafe and that's where I think the dis-ease started to develop. Hubby gave up his government job to work FIFO in the mines and whether I like to believe it or not I started to develop anxiety, well I think it was always there without a doubt it just escalated with being the only parent on site per se and running a business I wanted to be perfect at, gah the word perfectionism haunts me!

'Perfectionism is the belief that if we live perfect, and act perfect, we can minimise or avoid the pain of blame judgment and shame. It's a shield.'
— Brené Brown

I have done my fair share of therapies to help me through over the years, although now I believe it was never deep enough, band aid therapy really. A few shrinks here and there, podcasts, books etc.

Yet nothing has ever made me feel the way chemotherapy has, in fact as I wrote this, I am on my eighteenth round. (December 2024)

In early 2023 life had become a bit hectic on a few more levels, I mean it had been for years without realising it, just escalated with hubby quitting his job in the mines which stressed me out immensely, we had business repayments, house mortgages, land repayments, car repayments and he decides home maintenance was a great idea and gone from earning a decent wage to earning a few hundred a week, my gut was churning for months, constant phone calls coming in asking why payments were late, constantly wondering when his new position would start covering all our bills, on top of that I was trying to run a business that was effected with the post-covid no staff situation so eighteen-hour days became a normal, son was falling asleep in class so I pulled him out of school and used him to help me at the cafe, I was constantly worrying about my daughter who had latched onto the new trend of self-harm, the calls from her school were literally gut wrenching and ironically always came in when I was driving, I would always have to stop to cry a river of tears in the car, every time thinking we had got over that hurdle she had found a new place to hide her pain, life became so heavy and I felt like I was drowning in all of it. I felt lonely, helpless, broke, exhausted and somehow alone.

In amongst all this I still managed to win businesswoman of the year, endless national and state awards and still smile on the daily, honestly, I don't know how I did it!

I had had enough of my husband saying, 'We'll be right, babe,' weve gotten through worse, but these days felt like they were the worst and without realising the stress was eating away at my body.

In June 2023 I was house sitting for my girlfriend and all of a sudden I felt like I had hit a wall, I know now that it was the first signs of cancer,

I mean I was always tired having worked the hours I was but this feeling was different, late on Thursday 13 July I was having a shower and felt a huge lump in the side of my right breast, I was a couple of gins down that night as I needed to take the edge of my exhaustingly busy day and was lathering the soap a way I never really had when I felt the lump, it felt so big, I remember yelling for my daughter to come and feel and tell me it was my imagination, she was sixteen and very well-versed in the teenage facial expressions so I knew it wasn't good.

On 14 July I rang my family GP and as he was away on holiday, I asked to see the best person for the situation, I was recommended a female GP who specialised in women's health, perfect right!?

Ahhh, no it wasn't, said GP rang me at work and asked if it was necessary to see her that day and asked what the problem was, I was a little taken back however expressed my concerns and she had me see her in the middle of lunch service, anyone in hospitality knows this isn't a good time but I closed my kitchen as I did not want to muck around with how large this lump felt. I was early for my appointment as was greeted with a 'this is very inconvenient to my day' attitude by said GP and without even sitting down to tell her about my lump, she had me sit on the side of a bed take my top and bra off and said, 'Where is it?' very abruptly!

I was in shock, she felt it for a maximum two seconds told me it was nothing sinister and said I could go back to work. Oh, and I had been dizzy too, so the recommendation for that was to get a new pillow! She also told me that she would refer me to get a mammogram, by 20 July (six days later) I had to organise my own.

I took myself off to Breast Screen WA, it was a 1pm appointment, the service there was beyond amazing, understanding and gentle, I remember seeing the lump on the screen and how enlarged my breast was and having a deep sinking feeling. After a weekend of worry my family GP of twelve years arrived back from holiday and I saw him on the Tuesday

25 July and told him of my concerns, he didn't even feel my lump he immediately rang the local sonographer/radiologist and I was booked into have an ultrasound within fifteen minutes, in his words, this was not a matter to wait!

When the radiologist/sonographer saw the lump, I had another gut sinking feeling, I was wondering why he was looking in my armpit area. By the time I had finished with the ultrasound late that afternoon I hadn't even made it to the car and Breast Screen WA called urging me to have an ultrasound, already done I said. The next morning Wednesday 25 July my family GP said it was urgent I have a biopsy, being I was in a small city no-one was available for weeks so I drove 500km and was booked in for a fine needle core biopsy at 11:30 the next day, 26 July, and OMG it hurt! Ice packs, ladies! I was black, blue and all sorts of colours sore for weeks.

On Friday 26 July, hubby takes me out for lunch to take my mind off things, and at 1:44pm before we had received our lunch my phone rang, it was my GP. I headed out front of the restaurant with a pit in my stomach and all I remember from a seven-minute phone call was 'malignant' just a mere twenty-four hours after my biopsy, for the thoroughness I was grateful. But my life changed in that moment, and I was so scared.

I was diagnosed with invasive ductal carcinoma, grade 2 HER2 positive breast cancer, an aggressive and hardworking (just like me) kind of cancer, and would have to start my treatment journey with neoadjuvant chemotherapy with herceptin.

Herceptin attaches to the hormone receptors on the breast cancer cells to stop the cells from growing and dividing, it also signals the immune system to destroy the cancer cells. Unfortunately for me the cells had spread to my lymph nodes. This led to six rounds of intensive chemotherapy every third week starting in September, and by God no matter how prepared I was, or how much trauma and pain I had already felt in my short forty-six years or how positive I had felt I was not prepared for the way it crippled me physically, emotionally or mentally.

On top of that intense six rounds of chemotherapy that had me in the mental status of wanting to be dead because I already felt like I was, I had fifteen rounds of radiation, surgeries, never-ending needles, scans and the constant getting my breasts out that I felt like dignity was out the door but the worst was the feeling, was feeling lonely.

Some days I have been unable to walk, talk, make it to the bathroom, move or even function in general, it was as if I was shedding my skin, and I am constantly trying to find the reason why me, instead of thinking why me if that makes sense, is this diagnosis a blessing and a curse? I have never wanted to live more than I do now, I have never appreciated life more than I do now, I have never lived and looked at life more than I do now, am I being reborn?

Is this diagnosis my wake-up call? Did I need this?

I know in my heart I know I had forgotten how to live, I was a women who worked, sometimes ate, drank copious amounts of coffee, slept and had that on repeat for far too long. I wasn't truly living.

My passion and purpose of being the best I could be in all areas of my life had led to my very detriment.

I am always searching within myself daily what I have to learn, where I went wrong and how I can do better with what has been for the past sixteen months, I believe I have learnt a lot of patience and understanding. Mostly for myself. Yet I still have so far to go and am ready for it.

My treatment journey isn't even over and daily I struggle yet I am still so grateful to be here, I want to take my story and somehow help others yet I am not sure yet as to how that might eventuate, however for now as long as I wake up daily, I am blessed, and the rest will follow.

My passion and purpose are to first and foremost survive this diagnosis, watch my babies become parents themselves, enjoy some travel, live fully with content.

I know my story isn't finished yet.

ABOUT MEL

Western Australian Perth-born my name is Melissa Homewood, I didn't have the most conventional of upbringings leading to an array of terrible circumstances as a teen/adult which led me to push down the pain of the past and make me to believe I had to strive for perfection in order to be loved or valued.

At the early age of sixteen I became an apprentice chef and was made employee of the month not long after.

At seventeen years of age a salad I created was in a magazine and I was apart of winning a Gold Plate award.

By nineteen I was qualified and running a restaurant and function centre.

By twenty-one I was head chef to the media and sponsors at The Sydney Olympics 2000.

By twenty-five I had my ultimate life dream and became a mum, months following straight back to work.

By thirty my dream of having my very own baby girl was answered and I continued to strive to be the best working mum I could be among all the other things life throws.

By my forties I had the perfect family and had successful businesses along the ways, accumulating things in life I thought we needed, houses, cars, holiday shack, rural blocks of land, award-winning business among a lot of other things somehow believing all these brought a sense of accomplishment and happiness.

My business represented not only what my passion was but also how I wanted to help others.

I got lost in working so much I forgot how to live and what life was truly about, alas I won a plethora of state and national awards in a short five years.

Then dis-ease came to teach me what life is really about and how stress, trauma, hurt, pain and resentment if not treated correctly can be detrimental not only to one mentally and emotionally but to one's physical being, sometimes we have to learn the hard way to be able to teach and help others.

Sometimes we have to have a million breakdowns to have one single breakthrough, at this stage of my forty-seven years of age I am still learning daily, most of all of late to appreciate life more than I ever have, its been the hardest and most excruciating lesson I have ever had to feel and learn.

If I have my way my new found love will be here for a while yet to help others along their way.

My new passion and purpose x

MICHAEL TELLIS
A JOURNEY TO FIND DEEP PURPOSE

School for me was without passion nor purpose. A low level of desire meant I approached school as something that had to be done; do the book work, listen to the teachers, get the grades, please all concerned. That is until I went to woodworking classes at a nearby technical school. That was fun and interesting, a hint of a profound interest, something I could be passionate about in the real world.

University was completely different. It was fun and I dreamt of living and working in North America or Europe. That dream grew into a burning desire. I wanted to take action and my passion for that dream drove my decision to become an accountant and work for an international accounting firm. A job offer from a local accounting firm was declined because it was not aligned to my dream to live in another country. Not only did I get to work in Calgary, Canada, but I also worked in London, and there I was offered a job which was beyond my dreams.

From our apartment in a converted spice warehouse, where you could smell the aroma of spices whenever it rained, walking twenty minutes to work in the city of London across the picturesque Tower Bridge, past the foreboding Tower of London and on to 20 Fenchurch Street (now the Walkie Talkie), being amongst all that history was surreal. The work was interesting and challenging, and the people wonderful. The universe delivered well beyond my expectations.

Looking back, that experience is my first recollection of how a burning desire and passionate actions toward an outcome, could deliver not just an outcome, but better than expected outcomes. At no stage from university to arriving in Calgary, Canada, did I doubt myself in achieving my desire of working in the profession of my choice in another country. It was my first realisation that if I truly wanted something, had an emotional connection to it and kept a singular focus, I could achieve that object of desire.

Step-by-little-step, a profound interest ignites an inquiring mind, one with an insatiable thirst for learning and yet another adventure on the journey. Passion for something keeps us on the path and guides us back when we stray, for stray I did when passion waned and interest was lukewarm.

The years after London were not much to write about, or so I then thought, and I recall them as the lost years, until the birth of my beautiful daughter. New challenges, new responsibilities and less appetite for risk, until the passion inside returned. An advertisement in 2002 for a car company had the line *Don't Die Wondering* – and it ignited a series of events.

With a new purpose evolving, the passion returned, new dreams were born, the universe called, and I realised it was time to pay attention and make changes. The universe showed me I was on my path again through synchronicity, that wonderful feeling of flow, of joy in the challenges, the experience of the journey.

So, it was time to leave the comfort of a secure and respectable job and start a business with my wife. A passion I thought we shared, but not so. Different areas of interest gave birth to two businesses and we eventually went our separate ways.

My new passion was to create an organisation bigger than me, something with impact, to fill a need not yet fulfilled. When you show devotion through inspired action, the Universe sends people to you to bring to life what you are passionate about. Shortly after making the decision to create a business, I received an invitation to meet with three people which started the reality of building *Think180*, the first dedicated SAP IT consultancy in our city. We achieved a lot in fourteen years before I sold my share in 2022 to take time out. The break was needed and a valuable investment of time for me to contemplate my journey, so far, and ask a most important question: *Why am I here?*

All through my life I never felt part of the traditional route – a fish out of water. With a love of business, roles in sales and account management, eventually, it was working with people and culture where I felt most at home. That was where my interest was sparked about the importance of mindset and I gladly went the extra mile researching and attending courses. Why did some people understand how to use imagination, one of the most powerful of all human skills, and bring their imagining into reality, whilst other people dream about obtaining more from life, but remain in the same situation, somewhat frustrated, unfulfilled, or even worse, not liking where they are?

Why was it that when I genuinely and passionately wanted something, when I had a burning desire, a purpose bigger than my then-reality, I was able to bring that new reality into life? But, when the passion was lukewarm, the result would also turn out to be lukewarm, ho-hum and timid. My research continued and a review of my life against a framework of newfound knowledge brought insights; a pattern emerged.

Powerful insights started when I enrolled in a neuro-linguistic programming (NLP) course in September 2014. While I had known about meditation, it was not until the NLP course that I began practicing meditation. That was the game changer in starting the journey of connecting with my higher self. Sitting in the quiet and listening to my higher self would eventually lead me to find my purpose.

Two books were recommended during the course: *You Can Heal Your Life* by Louise Hay, and *Money and the Law of Attraction* by Esther and

Jerry Hicks.

Your thoughts impact your health. We live in a vibrational universe and the supply of abundance is unlimited. You must ask with passion for what you want. Now the journey to opening my heart and leaving the noise of my analytical mind behind was well under way. The best was yet to come, however, as is often the case with major change, the worst had to happen first.

The worst manifested in the form of a major relationship breakup. Ripping open my heart chakra provided me the choice to either cover the pain with substances or go deep and find out who I really am. Thanks to my sister recommending a life coach, I chose to go deep and do the inner work.

Nicole, who I worked with for nine years, was critical to my awakening into a universe of infinite possibilities, as well as learning and applying self-development tools and techniques beyond those offered at school and in my corporate environment.

Reading, listening, meditating, telling yourself, *'One day I will,'* is daydreaming of a better life. The *force is with you* only if you take inspired action and develop belief in yourself. If you don't yet believe in yourself, Cliona O'Hara, founder of the Napoleon Hill Institute, suggests borrow someone's belief in you, until you do.

A new passion slowly emerged as I explored the concept of *'change your mindset, change your life'*.

The change was not immediate as my behaviours and activities of the previous decades were held deep. My role in the business continued but slowly new practices were introduced to my daily routine of work and life. Meditation and affirmations to rewire my neural pathways soon became a daily practice, assisted by buying a house in the foothills surrounded by trees and quiet.

I was blessed with koalas walking past my front door, foxes on the driveway looking for the stray chickens and chopping wood for the glass-fronted wood heater which warmed the house on those cold days. Focusing on those dancing flames provided an ideal start to a meditation.

The journey to the heart was a quiet one, as it was gradual; a very slow awakening. Very slow because it was so different from how I understood the world worked and how life should be lived. While I was born in India, the world of yoga, yogis, reincarnation, the spiritual path and Ayurvedic medicine were not discussed in my early years as we were part of the European-Indian community. Descendants of the Catholic Portuguese, Dutch and French, we spoke English, products of the last vestiges of the British Raj.

Had I stayed in India, things might have been different, but the family moved to Australia when I was six years old and, apart from the delicious food, which was a welcome new cuisine in Australia in the 1970s, Indian culture was left behind. School, church, university and finding a good job were the focus and I embraced the world of business, devouring books on Jimmy Goldsmith, Rubert Murdoch and Kerry Packer.

The analytical mind is not bad, just different to the joy of working with your heart energy and leaving the restrictions of the logical mind behind. The years with my life coach were important for insights into how my energy body works, learning reiki and higher healing techniques using crystal singing bowls and those skills, tools and daily practices eventually tipped the scales. Eventually, because it took years to break through to the real me. The devotion to finding the real me was starting to pay off. Passionate learning yes but no purpose; no personally meaningful long-term goal that would make a positive mark on the world.

There is a saying; '*The master cannot teach until the student is ready to learn.*' In a similar vein, I would like to suggest that the universe cannot assist until the person wants to awaken.

Important steps on the journey to the real me were forgiveness and gratitude.

Forgiveness to myself for all the things I should have or could have done, and forgiveness to everyone who I felt had wronged me in some small or big way. It included ending life contracts that no longer served a purpose on my journey forward. Forgiveness allowed me to let go of baggage I had been carrying for years.

Gratitude provided me with a lift in frequency through a deep appreciation of what I had, from the simple things to the significant, and it opened a door to a sense of peace I had not felt before. Giving gratitude daily, changed the way I viewed the world and opened my eyes to the beauty in all things, from small flowers in the paddocks to the glow and joy in a smile, to the wealth around me. It all took time and deliberate actions every day were the key to opening the door to my new self.

The journey to self was a new passion because to this point in my life, I did not know what a journey was! I was focused on the destination. There is only one stage of my life I can recall when I truly understood that the journey is what's important, and that was back when I lived in Calgary and London. Time stood still each day so I could enjoy the moment, and each new day brought a new experience, a journey of wonder.

It was only when I sold my share in the business, had total flexibility in my day, my mother passed (at ninety-nine years and four months), my heart ripped again and I went into more intense healing, and much deeper inner work, that the heart opened and I could walk with my higher self. It was a massive year of self-discovery starting in July 2022. A life purpose was slowly unfolding as I walked this new path.

My poem below captures how I now go about my life, connecting with my higher self and trusting the universe. Being aware each day of opportunities for living a full and better life.

The Journey said come with me
For I will show you things you will remember many years from now
And I will cause you to remember things from many years from now
You may ask, Is this magic?

And I will answer, No it is not.
For this is you my love
And I will whisper these wisdoms in your ear
As you travel with me on this path to the Light
This awakening to You
And when you realise the Light is inside of You
Shining bright
You and I will merge my love
We will be the Light
And then You will not need to wonder anymore
For We will be the Journey evermore

A few years before my full awakening, I needed to find a new home. It was a fantastic opportunity to see if I could use my new-found tools and insights to manifest my dream home on a few acres of land. Burning desire, manifestation mantras, meditation, holding the emotion of living in this home, visualisation, writing down exactly what I wanted and taking action to search and attend open house inspections resulted in … guess what? I found the home I had asked for, but the universe again delivered beyond expectations; rainwater tanks, an olive grove, views of the vines and the ancient Willunga Hills, with bonus views of the coast and an almond grove.

Now it was time for that important part of living a full life, time to step up, listen to my higher self and contemplate a deep purpose, a legacy. That is how the *Numente Framework* was conceived. It is a step-by-step guide to achieve all twelve riches of life, even those riches you only dream about. It led me to my purpose; to guide and support people to find and live their purpose, and connect with their higher selves.

Please take a moment to imagine how wonderful the world would be if we all had the knowledge and skills to live an abundant life. To feel worthy, to ask for and acquire our share of all twelve riches of life through application of universal laws, equitable principles and sound habits.

How did this framework arise? How did my purpose unfold?

As I told my story of personal growth to the people I mentored and coached, formally, informally and in general conversations, I was encouraged to keep researching and applying the knowledge. The more I found out, the more I realised there was so much more to learn. More to learn about me and these magical insights. And why were these insights, many well-articulated in the 1920s to 1950s, not taught in school? Wouldn't we all be better off living our dreams and not be a slave to someone else's dream?

In 2019, during a conversation about these powerful insights, one of the team at *Think180* suggested I capture and share these learnings and insights. Taking a long break after I left *Think180* provided the perfect opportunity to consolidate my thoughts on how the universe works, how you can achieve anything your heart truly desires and how your future can be so much better than your current reality. And that was how the framework was born.

Find a purpose, maintain your passion, learn how to overcome your fears and doubts, stay devoted to the path and the universe will send you the resources and people you need.

A person with passion and purpose is unstoppable.

ABOUT MICHAEL

With a professional background as a chartered accountant, living in different countries and co-founding *Think180*, a successful IT consulting practice, Michael found he lived a fulfilled life when he had a purpose bigger than him. While his purpose changed over the decades, the pattern was consistent. Life without purpose was unfulfilling and he drifted, but when he had a purpose bigger than him, life flowed and had meaning and excitement.

His role leading people and culture at *Think180* sparked a deep interest in exploring these concepts and if a better understanding could help others live more fulfilling lives.

His research revealed that when it comes to what people desire most in life, mental and physical wellbeing is paramount to maintaining a high quality of life. And he concluded from his personal experience that purpose and mindset are the foundations for achieving wellbeing.

Through this journey, Michael found his big purpose in guiding and supporting people to find their purpose and build their mindset and habits to bring that purpose to life.

Accordingly, today Michael focuses on working with people through the lens of his Numente Framework, breaking down personal growth into manageable steps and developing plans for people to transition from surviving to thriving and living a fulfilling life. The framework guides people one step at a time until they are ready for the big leaps. It is a practical step-by-step guide which simplifies some of the complexities of personal development.

Michael developed the framework after he left *Think180*, at which time he also gained his coaching certification through the Napoleon Hill Institute. This dynamic organisation, based in New York, has a rigorous program for certification based on the principles of *Think and Grow Rich* by Napoleon Hill, a foundational book in self-development. His skills to help others have been enriched by working with a life coach for many years to develop his understanding of our energy body, power of meditation and ancient wisdom.

Michael is steadfast in his commitment and passion for empowering others to realise their limitless potential, through an individual's connection to both a worthwhile purpose and a strong mindset.

His greatest joy is to see people transition from living a life in which they feel they are surviving day-to-day, to living a life in which they are thriving and feel fulfilled.

For those interested in exploring the Numente Framework or working with Michael as a coach, he invites you to connect and start the journey toward unlocking your limitless potential.

MIKE MACKAY
PENNING EXISTENCE

There are as many reasons for writing as there are for not writing. Ultimately, what separates those who write from those who don't is not necessarily the strength of their feelings or ideas but rather the interplay of factors like opportunity, confidence, external support and personality. Writing often requires a unique combination of circumstances, motivation and commitment.

Why do you write? What purpose drives your authorship and storytelling? What passion drives you to transpose your thoughts and mental movies into words?

One possible purpose is to connect – to create a shared experience that resonates with readers and bridges the gap between individuals. Through your storytelling, you can evoke empathy and understanding, fostering a sense of connection that transcends boundaries.

Another purpose may be to grapple with questions, articulate emotions and delve into themes that matter to you. It's a journey of discovery, both for yourself and your audience.

Yet another purpose might be to inspire and provoke thought. Stories can challenge assumptions, ignite curiosity and encourage readers to see the world in new ways. They can catalyse change, whether on a personal or broader societal scale.

Ultimately, your purpose may be a unique combination of these elements. But where does the passion come from?

HEAR US ROAR: TIGER EDITION

Let us examine the background and opportunities of some great authors, to understand better the concepts of *Passion and Purpose*.

J R R Tolkien graduated with first-class honours at Oxford in 1915, but his academic pursuits were interrupted by the outbreak of World War I. His experiences in the trenches, particularly during the Battle of the Somme, left a lasting impression on him and influenced the themes of loss, heroism, and camaraderie that permeate his writing.

He created stories for his four children, including *The Hobbit*, which began as a bedtime tale before evolving into a literary masterpiece.

His Catholic faith imbued his writing with moral clarity and spiritual depth. At the same time, his experiences in World War I and his observations of the industrialisation of England informed his portrayal of the destructive forces of greed and power.

J K Rowling grew up in a modest household. She began writing stories as a young girl, including one about a rabbit named "Rabbit" when she was six.

Her mother's diagnosis of multiple sclerosis and death instilled in her a sense of empathy and resilience that would later influence her writing.

The idea for *Harry Potter* came to Rowling in 1990 during a delayed train journey from Manchester to London.

The *Harry Potter* series draws on various influences, including mythology, folklore, and classical literature. Rowling's background in the Classics is evident in the Latin-based spells and the mythological creatures that populate her magical world.

Her portrayal of prejudice, inequality, and the abuse of power resonates with readers.

Jane Austen and her family lived modestly. The household was intellectually vibrant, filled with books, lively discussions, and a shared love of storytelling.

Austen's formal education was brief, typical for girls of her social class at the time.

Her father's death in 1805 forced the Austen women to rely on the support of Jane's brothers.

It wasn't until 1809, when the Austen women settled in a cottage, that she resumed her writing in earnest. She revised her earlier manuscripts and wrote new works.

Marriage served as a personal and societal lens to critique the financial and social pressures placed on women. Her characters' choices, whether guided by love, duty, or ambitions, reflect the complexities of navigating societal expectations.

Fyodor Mikhailovich Dostoevsky's father was a doctor at a hospital for the poor, and his mother was a deeply religious woman. The contrast between his father's stern temperament and his mother's gentle religiosity shaped Dostoevsky's perception of authority, morality and compassion.

When Dostoevsky was fifteen, his mother died of tuberculosis. Despite his disinterest in a military career, he attended the Nikolayev Military Engineering Institute in St. Petersburg.

In 1844, Dostoevsky resigned from his military post to pursue a literary career. In 1849, the Tsarist government arrested him for his involvement in the Petrashevsky Circle, whose ideas were considered subversive. His sentence was death by firing squad. On the day of his execution, at the last moment, the sentence was commuted to four years of hard labour in Siberia.

After his release from prison in 1854, as part of his sentence, Dostoevsky served in the military. During this time, he married his first wife, Maria Dmitrievna Isaeva, a woman who suffered from tuberculosis and whose volatile personality added to Dostoevsky's emotional turmoil. The couple's relationship was fraught with challenges, including Dostoevsky's struggles with epilepsy and gambling addiction, which led to significant financial debts.

George Orwell was born into a middle-class family in Motihari, Bengal, British India. The family lived modestly.

Orwell attended St. Cyprian's Preparatory School, where he experienced the British educational system's rigid class consciousness and harsh discipline. From St. Cyprian's, Orwell earned a scholarship to Eton College.

After Eton, Orwell joined the Indian Imperial Police in Burma (now Myanmar) in 1922. During his time in Burma, he began questioning the British Empire's moral legitimacy and the corrosive effects of colonialism. In 1927, Orwell resigned from the Indian Imperial Police and returned to England, determined to become a writer.

Upon returning to England, Orwell embarked on a period of self-imposed hardship, living among the working poor in London and Paris. Orwell's immersion in the lives of the poor reflected his growing belief that the writer's role was to bear witness to suffering and speak truth to power. He rejected the literary elitism of his time, insisting that writing should serve as a tool for social change. This commitment to social justice became a hallmark of his work.

Harper Lee was born in Monroeville, Alabama, and was the youngest of four children. Her father was a lawyer and newspaper editor. Her father's career and moral convictions had a significant influence on her.

Monroeville was a quintessential Southern town, marked by the rigid racial and social hierarchies of the Jim Crow era, but also a place of community and storytelling, where the oral traditions of the South played a significant role in shaping her literary voice.

After college, Lee moved to New York City to pursue her literary ambitions. She worked various jobs while dedicating herself to her craft.

The genesis of *To Kill a Mockingbird* began in the 1950s, when Lee's friends, recognising her talent, provided financial support so she could write full-time. This generosity allowed Lee to focus on her novel, drawing inspiration from her childhood experiences in Monroeville and her observations of Southern society.

C S Lewis was born into a comfortable middle-class family in Belfast.

His father was a solicitor, and his mother was highly educated and instilled in him a love of reading and learning. Tragically, Lewis's mother passed away from cancer when he was just nine years old, an event that profoundly affected him and contributed to his later struggles with faith.

After his mother's death, Lewis and his brother, Warren, were sent to boarding schools in England. His experiences at these schools were often harsh and lonely.

Lewis was a gifted student, which led him to study at University College, Oxford. His education was interrupted by World War I, during which he served as a second lieutenant in the British Army. The horrors of war deepened his skepticism of religion and solidified his atheistic beliefs.

During this period, Lewis was an outspoken atheist. However, his intellectual rigor and curiosity led him to question and eventually abandon his atheism.

Lewis became one of the most eloquent and influential defenders of the Christian faith, using his literary talents and sharp intellect to articulate complex theological ideas in an accessible and engaging manner, such as *The Chronicles of Narnia*.

Virginia Woolf was born into an intellectually vibrant and socially prominent family. Her father was a distinguished literary critic and historian. Her mother was known for her beauty, philanthropy, and connections to well-known artists and intellectuals of the time. Educated at home, she grew up in a household steeped in literature and culture.

The deaths of her mother in 1895, her half-sister Stella in 1897, and her father in 1904 had a profound impact on her mental health. These losses contributed to the bouts of depression and mental illness that would affect her throughout her life.

Despite these challenges, she remained remarkably productive, channeling her emotions into her writing. However, the onset of World War II and the destruction it brought to England weighed heavily on her.

On 28th March 1941, Woolf took her own life by drowning in the River Ouse near her home in Sussex. She left behind a poignant note to her husband, expressing her love and gratitude.

Agatha Christie was born into a well-to-do family. Her father was an American stockbroker, and her mother was an Englishwoman. Agatha spent her early years in a comfortable Victorian household, where she was encouraged to cultivate her imagination and creativity. Her mother, in particular, played a significant role in shaping her love of storytelling.

Christie did not receive formal schooling in her early years. She was educated at home by her mother and governesses, who fostered an environment where young Agatha could dream and invent tales.

Agatha's journey into writing began during World War I when she worked as a nurse at a hospital in Torquay and later as a dispenser in the hospital pharmacy.

Christie's legacy is inseparable from her two most iconic creations: Hercule Poirot and Miss Jane Marple. These characters exemplify her talent for creating unforgettable detectives with distinct personalities and methods.

Her two most famous characters embody different facets of Christie's storytelling: Hercule Poirot represents logical deduction and intellectual rigor, while Miss Marple highlights intuition and moral insight.

Gabriel García Márquez was born into a modest family in Colombia. His maternal grandparents primarily raised him and played a profound role in shaping his imagination and worldview.

His grandfather was a storyteller who regaled young García Márquez with tales of war, love and political intrigue. His grandmother spoke of omens, premonitions, and other supernatural occurrences as if they were part of everyday life. This blending of the real and the fantastic became a hallmark of García Márquez's literary style and was the foundation for his later exploration of magical realism.

He studied law at the National University of Colombia, however, he soon abandoned his legal studies to pursue a career in journalism and writing. His early experiences as a journalist took him to other parts of the world, exposing him to diverse cultures and ideas that enriched his storytelling. His work in journalism also honed his ability to craft precise and evocative narratives. A skill that would characterize his fiction.

García Márquez is often considered a pioneer of magical realism, a literary style that infuses the mundane with the extraordinary and allows the fantastical to coexist with the real. However, he did not consider magical realism an invention – it was simply how he saw and experienced life, especially in Latin America.

Margaret Eleanor Atwood was born in Ottawa, Ontario, Canada. Her childhood was unique, as she spent her time mainly in the remote wilderness of Northern Quebec, where her entomologist father conducted field research.

Atwood had limited access to formal education and modern conveniences, however, her parents were intellectual and supportive, fostering her curiosity and love for books.

She attended the University of Toronto, earning a Bachelor of Arts in English, with minors in philosophy and French, in 1961. Atwood later pursued postgraduate studies at Harvard University, where her studies gave her a deeper appreciation of history, particularly the recurring patterns of power and oppression, which became central themes in her novels.

Writing during a time of great societal upheaval, Atwood became a keen observer of gender inequalities and the societal systems that perpetuated them. Her novel *The Handmaid's Tale* (1985), one of her most celebrated works, reflects this focus. Set in a dystopian future, the story serves as both a cautionary tale and a critique of patriarchal structures. Atwood's observations of historical and contemporary examples of systemic oppression and her study of Puritanical religious practices in New England were the inspiration.

Mike Mackay: Which brings us back to me. My bio reads as follows.

Mike has always wanted to tell stories, possibly due to his predominantly Irish Heritage. These stories have taken many forms: novels, short stories, poems, and spoken. They are now seeing the light of day via his publisher.

He has a masters degree in computer science. As an independent contractor in the software industry, he has created businesses, owned a five-star game farm and a one-star pub, driven trucks for his horse transport business, worked for a gangster, made money, lost money, and made it again. This journey enabled him to see the good, the bad, and the ugly in the context of the seven deadly sins. He has worked on every continent and every business sector.

He is a fisherman, a hunter, a surfer, a water skier, a scuba diver, a polocrosse player, a black belt karateka, a tournament fighter and a daily writer in his journal.

He has been married three times and has five biological children, three step-children and eight grandchildren. They live in England, South Africa, Australia and China.

Mike now lives back in the land of his birth, Australia, in a renovated house on a beach in Western Australia.

The eleven people I have summarised in the previous pages are a mixed bag of cultures, continents, locales, backgrounds, and stories they are compelled to tell. Imagine for a moment having them all in the same room, even for just one hour, to ask them what is the passion that drives authorship and what is its purpose. The purpose of each of the individuals I have mentioned is clear, but the question of where the passion comes from to put words on a page is like asking air where it came from. It just is.

When I meet people who don't write, I wonder what is that match within me that strikes the side of the matchbox, which creates a spark, then a flame which, when put with combustible material, produces a fire that does not want to go out.

MIKE MACKAY

I think Gabriel García Márquez got it right when he said, 'Everyone has three lives; a public life, a private life and a secret life.' Writing often emerges as the medium through which individuals explore and share their secret lives, those innermost thoughts, dreams, and fears that might otherwise go unspoken. For those who feel driven to give a voice to these hidden aspects of themselves, writing becomes not just a choice but a necessity to put in writing what is in their secret lives.

ABOUT MIKE

Mike has always wanted to tell stories, possibly due to his predominantly Irish heritage. These stories have taken many forms: novels, short stories, poems and spoken. They are now seeing the light of day via his publisher.

He has a masters degree in computer science. As an independent contractor in the software industry, he has created businesses, owned a five-star game farm and a one-star pub, driven trucks for his horse transport business, worked for a gangster, made money, lost money, and made it again. This enabled him to see the good, bad, ugly and the impact of the seven deadly sins. He has worked on every continent and every business sector.

He is a fisherman, a hunter, a surfer, a water skier, a scuba diver, a polocrosse player, a black belt karateka, a tournament fighter and a daily writer in his journal.

He has worked on every continent and every business sector.

He has been married three times and has five biological children, three step-children and eight grandchildren. They live in England, South Africa, Australia and China.

Mike now lives back in the land of his birth, Australia, in a renovated house on a beach in Western Australia.

NICOLE WHITTY
THE DREAM

The dream was always the same – a memory from another time, seeing myself with him in another body; different face and place but the same soul.

On a mountain top sheltered by an old tree, I knew we met there often.

It was our place. Sitting together, with no words, just a resonance of belonging. One with abundant beauty everywhere, feeling none of it mattered without him.

We were wearing native clothes, as it was just us. I was his, he was mine; that moment etched in our hearts for eternity. The tree where we would come together as friends, lovers. Knowing my soul knew his, for lifetimes.

The energetic imprint of being there with him in that memory would stay with me throughout the day, as the dream recurred repeatedly. I didn't know who he was in this life, yet beyond the enigma, my soul knew his energy, knew his heart and knew he was special; the one who felt like home. I would go to the beach and look across the far horizon, feeling he was out there *somewhere*.

At times, I was content being by myself. I didn't want superficial connections or shallow interactions with anyone. If I did have another partner in this life, it had to be different from my past. I wanted authentic, trustworthy, kind, loving people around me.

After a very painful breakup, I didn't want to be hurt again. I was protecting myself for a while because of what I'd been through, so when

I had these dreams, I didn't want to assume anything. I was used to keeping everyone at a distance. Although I'd always been very loving and friendly to everyone and I'd tried not to close my heart, betrayal and not being able to trust during a previous relationship, had closed it shut for some time. Out of self-preservation, I felt I had no choice. It hurt like hell, so I decided to only give this love to a few and work through my feelings the best I could. I was in my early twenties and didn't know how else to respond.

I wanted to be loved, as we all do, but I wasn't facing myself. In fact, I was running away from myself. Studying and trying to work out my own trauma, my feelings would hit me like a ton of bricks. One thing I did do though, was meditate daily and consistently, asking the divine mother and father to guide me. It's so interesting when we do this, because random things arise, like thoughts, reactions and catalysts that open realisations; we don't know they are the answers to what we have asked until all the pieces come together.

As the coming together of our souls was approaching, he would be the catalyst to reopening my heart and having many realisations beyond my 'me' world. The closer I got to reuniting with him, the more visions and dreams were happening. I was reliving the memories we had shared in other lifetimes together, both emotionally and energetically. Later, the dots would join, and it would all make sense. Throughout my life, I had always had these visions, knowing when I met people in person – but not like this; this was different.

The reason I'm reflecting on this memory, is because each of us has many purposes we explore, that reveal our growth, often inspired by those we love. Souls that change our lives can reach parts of ourselves we didn't even know were there. We are drawn like a magnet yet can't explain it. We trust them in ways we have never shared with another person outside of our family before.

With billions of people in the world, I have often wondered, *why that person?*

These soul ties are so profound because we have known these souls for many lifetimes.

Friendship and love between souls is built up over those lifetimes. That's why we naturally click with some people and feel we've known them forever, even when we first meet, while others we never think about or want to see again. Some, we have an instant dislike for and can't put our finger on why. We sell ourselves the story to justify our feelings and feel, at our core, that our reasoning is valid. Maybe it is true - maybe we are seeing the truth of that person, maybe not.

I always find it interesting when someone has said something innocuous or done nothing wrong, but we instantly dislike them. On a soul level, it does imply memories within that are being revealed for growth to take place. Everyone is a catalyst for us to see ourselves, our thinking, feelings and beliefs that we are running on.

However, because most of us don't remember our other lifetimes, why would we know or even consider the truth within it? The reason is, because we are in the now, the present moment, which is our most empowered state to create from. If we are always focusing on the past, we simply are not in the present moment. We must be aware though, that everything from every lifetime, all the work we have done on ourselves spiritually, everything we have offered ourselves, others and the world, everything we have believed or felt, is in our subconscious as energy. So, the answers to our *why?* questions are in these other lifetimes, and we only seem to access them if we are meant to, or allowed to.

These feelings, or reactions, happen spontaneously, without us consciously trying to force it. When we break it all down to the beginning of everything, it is all energy and frequency; sound with data on it. The real question is: *What is going on at a deeper soul level, when we have these memory triggers that catapult us into specific energetic, physical, emotional, mental experiences, decisions, discussions, actions and perceptions?*

HEAR US ROAR: TIGER EDITION

Soul recognition and the purpose of it, comes with an energy that has encoded information being experienced through our senses, our body, our mind, our programming and our level of awareness, accumulated over many lifetimes, as filters. The passion, frequency discharge, that is expelled from our beings when this recognition occurs is mind-blowing, especially when it is a soul we have loved for lifetimes. It's exciting; we love seeing them. We have met the one we have searched for in others and when they appear, we know them.

We want to be with them.

We are drawn to them.

We are attracted to them.

To be aware that these intimate connections between souls are created over lifetimes is profound and makes so much sense. This helped me to understand love and friendship on another level, through *him* as a catalyst, to move from my past assumptions and more into love. Especially when I had made up my mind I was going to meet my soul mate; a soul that I could experience *true love* with.

Within two weeks, he walked straight into the shop where I was working and stayed for hours talking. The soul recognition was instant. We were drawn to one another, and so, the walls in my heart had to come down. That was quite hard, I must admit. Mainly because I was stubborn and still had issues I needed to resolve – things I didn't even know were there until I loved someone like this.

When you love someone so much, all the fears and memories *that aren't love* arise, and we do all we can to try to prevent feeling those negative emotions again. Yet for true love to be explored, *all that is not love* must dissolve. The part of us that needs to defend, protect ourselves and project the past into the now, needs to die. If we want it.

So, I was at the bottom of the victim stairs that I had created myself in my own heart, and I had to let it all go – if I wanted him. If I wanted love. If I wanted to remember what it was like to be love and to actually feel more joy.

As I was to find out, he would be my greatest teacher.

For all that I rejected within myself, he loved, accepted and never judged. Just kept loving me, no matter how much I tried to protect myself from the very thing that was being offered to set me free. The opportunity was given, and I had to decide whether I would let myself receive it. Instead of criticising and finding reasons not to be happy, I decided I would ask myself,

'How can I be more loving today?'

'How can I encourage and bring harmony to this moment?'

Did I always get it right? No. I didn't.

I was learning each time I was practicing this. Every time, I had to get over myself to have another realisation of another dimension to love and what it might mean, without setting it in concrete. Focusing on the vibration of it as a *knowing* instead. Letting go of what I thought things were, to be open to see what was.

The longer we were together, I felt I could share more with him of what I had experienced leading up to us meeting. I told him about my dreams I'd had of him before we united.

He'd had the same dream. He knew exactly what I was describing; the tree, us being together, everything. He too had sat at the beach, thinking the same thing as I had. We were already in sync as our soul's came closer and closer to meeting once again.

With this, came many initiations together, some deeply testing, then absolutely beautiful; true acceptance and love of one another, blossoming with each inner hurdle we held one another through. If I hadn't had these moments, I wouldn't have accumulated understanding and compassion for others, nor myself. The moments where I felt devalued, were opportunities for me to love myself, as I am, and decide my value without putting it in another person's hands. *The gift within everything is revealed when we meet everything with love.*

Going beyond the horizon of needing validation and approval, is surrendering to the experience of learning from one another through love. Communing with another world that sees through different eyes, is not needing to be right, or for them to be anything other than what they are, infatuated by the distinctive essence that is moulded into that one soul.

From this experience I became aware that although we have a certain amount of time together on Earth, our love lasts forever. Beyond this life within our souls. It doesn't die. Our impermanent physical forms leave, but the soul's heart remembers. The love feels like God; it is a quality of the pure consciousness that we all are, that we give as a donation, a quality of consciousness to the collective of all, to remind us the love we feel for one another, that we seek in everything externally, is already inside of us.

It is the quality of love that allows the magic to light the fire that perpetuates the propulsion of energy to create everything in life. Opened by a catalyst, to show us all that is not love, to explore what it is. This stimulates thoughts, perspectives and emotions to decide what we want, to make decisions, to create as we build our lives around those we love. We become motivated to learn how to give this love and compassion to ourselves by offering it to others.

We do so many things based on those we love and the quality of our relationships.

Some relationships are for life, others for a time for whatever reason, and then you have those who blow in and blow out, like leaves carried by the wind. Each association has its purpose, whether positive, neutral or negative. Soul growth is experienced with all, when we meet everything with love, understanding and compassion.

We share the creation of our lives through the energy of love, to recognise that when we do, the results are distinctly different to when we create from destruction. If we were all creating from love, which is creation energy, the abundant frequency of life, imagine the world we would live in? It's a dissolving of separation within ourselves, grown from what we access through true heartfelt, authentic relations with others; enjoying one another, seeing the good in each other, encouraging, supporting one another, being there for each other.

This moves us beyond the atrocities that are prolific in human history. Beyond indoctrination into ideologies that allow and justify the opposite of love. Evolving from separation consciousness in society, the family home, in relationships, the way we relate to and perceive ourselves, one another, the world. Stepping out of the dark and into the heart, where love is underneath all that is not love. Transcending limited states of consciousness to remember and take back our power to choose and create the lives we wish to live.

In harmony with the earth, with all living beings for the benefit of all.

There is enough for everyone.

The souls we have built loving rapports with for many lifetimes, remind us of this love inside ourselves, as well as the cherished realisation that this is not just for our favourite people. This love is meant for us to embody and give, to all, through being it; wishing all well, wishing everyone good health, success, love, happiness, joy. Never investing our attention, our energy, our thoughts or emotions on hate, destruction, persecuting, condemning, jealousy, harm or division, as we know what these levels of awareness and intentions have done in the past. We know never to participate in it on any level, because these things are not love. The resounding echoes of the effects these choices create for generations, is enough for us to choose love.

This gift is expressed through respect for each other, understanding all are here to learn, grow and love through their filters, and need the space to do this without condemnation, but with understanding and compassion. So many of us want this freedom, to be ourselves, yet for you to have it, this freedom must be given to everyone, to everything.

We are at the precipice of the great awakening of all of humanity, and it only takes a small percentage of souls to truly be a living example, not just mentally, but emotionally vibrationally of love, for the universal law of critical mass to kick in.

For this love, respect, authenticity and reverence for all life to ripple through the collective consciousness, is for each soul to wake up from the subconscious limited programs of separation they are in. Which is the cause of all suffering, and ironically, the foundation from which all awakening stems. This is what we are evolving from, remembering the purpose of true soul relationships that are based in love.

The catalyst, the soul, the love, is a tapestry of devotion, woven into the fabric of life, expanding through the whole collective consciousness of humanity, bringing the intelligence of life itself to all that are open to receiving it. To see, with smiling eyes and hearts, the wonders that are all around us from embodying the qualities of love. The light ignites and our passion, purpose is delivered to create greatness for all to access.

For all to benefit, all to prosper, all to flow with life.

It starts with you, it starts with me; all of us contributing to the whole.

This is what his love consummated within my heart, to realise it isn't just about me. That whatever I am, whatever you are, is offered to the world vibrationally as an elixir to flourish or diminish life.

So, I ask myself, 'How can I be more loving today?'

ABOUT NICOLE

Nicole is the founder and CEO of the Elysian Sanctuary – Holistic Centre for Peace & Wellbeing in the Adelaide Hills of South Australia.

Nicole is a fully qualified SKHM Seichim master, Karuna master, reiki master teacher, quantum wnergy healer, intuitive medium and has been in service for the past fifteen years helping thousands of people from all over Australia and overseas with these abilities and is a meditation teacher, sound medicine healer and event, retreat facilitator for clients at the Elysian Sanctuary.

She is also a NHI global master coach offering online events to expand consciousness and assists people with creating their best lives through her Mindset for Wellbeing program – YOUR VISION FOR YOUR LIFE!

Always using her skills she offers in alignment with the laws of nature, to help others for the benefit of all, on all levels of consciousness. Everything she does is altered to the specific needs of each person or group she works with for optimum results.

As Nicole's reputation grew over the years from getting fabulous results with her clients, she always operated by word of mouth and letting universal intelligence guide what she does.

Recently being guided to serve globally, she has embarked on now being an author and sharing her stories with the world.

She can be contacted through email: whittyart@hotmail.com or +61403055825

You can find her on FB: facebook.com/Holistic.Intuitive.Healing

ROBYN VERRALL
FUELLED BY PASSION, DRIVEN BY PURPOSE

Passion is the fire that fuels action, and purpose is the direction that turns that fire into meaningful impact. For me, these two forces have been inseparable, shaping every step of my journey in love, agriculture, leadership and storytelling.

Our first love is often a fire that burns brightly; an undeniable intensity that consumes the heart and soul. It is passion in its purest form – an all-encompassing energy that drives us to experience life more deeply. Every glance, every touch and every moment feels magnified, charged with an excitement that seems limitless. First love is often reckless, uninhibited by fear or doubt, driven solely by the power of raw emotion.

Yet, most first love carries a sense of purpose, even if we don't recognise it at the time. It teaches us about ourselves – our desires, our vulnerabilities and our capacity for deep connection. It shapes the way we view relationships and sets the foundation for how we love in the future. Though it may not always last, as mine didn't, first love leaves an indelible mark, a lesson in what it means to truly give and receive love. I still recall elements of this with fondness and a deep sense of thanks.

Like passion and purpose in other areas of life, first love is most profound when it has direction. When love is nurtured with intention and mutual respect, it grows into something enduring, something that influences us long after the initial fire cools. It is in the lessons of first love that we often find the wisdom to approach future relationships with a greater sense of purpose, understanding that true love is not just about intensity but about commitment, growth and shared dreams.

First love is unique and can never be repeated, but every love that follows carries echoes of that initial passion and commitment. The way you love and connect with others is shaped by those early experiences. With each relationship, whether a fleeting encounter or one that lasts for months or years, we learn more about our desires, needs and purpose.

When we leave our first love or any to others to follow behind, we also leave behind its innocence – no matter how intense, good or bad it was. Mine was good. Yet, moving on often brings a mix of regret and sadness, and in some cases, excitement. When we leave these relationships, though anger and hurt may sometimes consume us, we must allow ourselves time to heal, to navigate adulthood and to enter new relationships without constantly measuring them against the first. When we reflect back, is it the person or the emotion we feel sad about leaving them behind? Or is it that we identify how we placed higher expectations on this person to love us back, with the same intensity, often more than they were incapable of? Do we then project the disappointment in ourselves on them? But once we learn to let go, we can forgive ourselves, embrace our mistakes and open our hearts to love again, ready for the next chapter of passion and purpose

Each time we enter a new connection, we seek the best in the other person, striving to be more honest, to express ourselves fully and to navigate the path ahead with clarity. And when you finally find the person with whom you want to build a life and family, you realise that passion's true purpose is not just in the spark but in the commitment; the intention to fully invest in the relationship and grow together.

My passion and purpose truly began after I met, and then married, my farmer; the man I reconnected with years later at our twenty-year high school reunion. Stepping into his world, unfamiliar and demanding as it was, ignited something deep within me, a deep love, not only for him, but for our land and for the people who dedicate their lives to feeding the world. My passion for agriculture didn't begin in childhood, (though I did have plenty of things shaped like cows!), it really began when I pulled up to his place and it felt as if I was *home* ... for the first time ever. It took me a while to realise it wasn't the house that was home, it was him.

What started as simply supporting my husband in *his* passion and purpose, soon became *my own*. I embraced the work, the challenges and the steep learning curve, guided by a man who never belittled my naive questions or made me feel out of place. He taught by showing, ensuring my safety, the animals' wellbeing and his own. Of course, some lessons weren't without a few heated words exchanged in the moment (swearing included) but that was just how we worked ... and still do. It was never personal, it was simply the nature of the job.

His patience, kindness and stamina were enough to fuel my own passion for the land. I soon realised that despite my past careers providing financial security, they had never truly given me a sense of purpose. Agriculture did.

Living and working alongside my husband, I quickly saw that he had forgotten more about farming than he'd ever have time to teach me. Yet, rather than feeling overwhelmed, this realisation only deepened my commitment. It was here, in this life we built together, that I truly found my voice.

I became the eyes, ears and advocate for our farming enterprise, carving out my own role and eventually creating a business within the farm itself. This not only gave me a sense of purpose beyond being an unpaid farmhand but also allowed me to contribute financially without needing to seek work outside of the farm. Maintaining my financial independence was important to me, as I had left a corporate sales career behind. So was having the flexibility to return to the city, reconnect with family and friends, and ensure I wasn't living in complete isolation. I had a mortgage to pay and desperately wanted to ensure I got to spend time with my daughter, who was living and studying in the city.

When I first started my business, selling affordable meats to family and friends, I quickly realised that many women in our society needed a hand up with access to nutritious and affordable food. Wanting to help, I reached out to my network to see who was in urgent need. I was surprised by the number of women I knew who contacted me and I discreetly delivered food to them. There was one who said her husband frowned on this action; her reaching out and me delivering. Her husband felt judged that he could not provide for his family, so it was stopped. I had to work out how to get her food without this blockage, and thus created a *pay it forward* option in the business. People would ask to donate the cost of the meat and then tell me they wanted it delivered to a family who needed a hand up. This solved the problem, as she could tell him it was paid for. Once they got back on their feet, they would then *pay it forward*. They did, and still do ten years later, to help others in the way we helped them.

Having the passion and the purpose to find a suitable solution without fear or favour, I began to advertise this, and we went from ad hoc deliveries to weekly, all the while, the stakeholders were able to get paid, so no one felt obligated, left out or dissatisfied with the process. It was here, two years into the business, that I met the most incredible women, all driven by the same passion and purpose.

With this mission at the heart of my business, I've aligned our farming efforts to make a real impact. I've had the privilege of working with remarkable organisations, including First Nations groups that support their communities through food, and we are fortunate to have built long-standing relationships with them.

I know that food is the solution to many things. It carries traditions, creates space for others, challenges cultural norms and opens more doors than ever before. When we have food, we have nourishment, connection and the power to foster community. It is more than sustenance, it is a bridge between cultures, a catalyst for conversation and a foundation for change.

I have stepped into homes where doors would not usually open, filled empty freezers and ensured they would never be empty again. This work has reinforced the power of connection, generosity and the importance of food security for all. Having been in food insecurity when I was a single mother, I identify with all people who feel marginalised and embarrassed. I tell people that 'pride' was the worst thing I owned! I felt I couldn't tell my amazing family and friends that, at the time, I was struggling to buy food. Now I share this story to illustrate my passion, which is driven to get affordable food onto the tables of vulnerable families, and gives me a deep sense of purpose to know I can assist them.

Once I stepped into the meat/farming business, I found that women in agriculture were often unseen and unheard, and I was at a real loss as to how to change this dynamic. In building my business and having my farmer husband working alongside me to promote me, my purpose became clear; to champion myself and women in agriculture to ensure they had a seat at the tables where decisions were made.

Here is an amazing community of clever, entrepreneurial, educated, talented women ready, willing and able to step up, sit down and contribute, yet all I saw was the lack of opportunities and difficulty navigating the farming family dynamics, unmet child care needs and lack of professional career options. This was combined with the obvious few misogynistic, *gatekeepers of the good old days*. We were, and still are, being held back and it needed a disruptor to start the change. I was that disruptor and have even been described as divisive, but I am passionate about change and know this is my purpose.

Purpose gives direction to passion. It is what drives me to push forward, to create opportunities and to challenge the status quo.

Becoming an advocate for women, not only in agriculture, wasn't just about speaking up, it was about opening doors, fostering connections and creating pathways for current and future generations. As I stepped into leadership roles, from business owner to one of AgriFutures Rural Women's Award Winner for South Australia, things began to change. I did so with the belief that representation matters, that every woman who dreams of making an impact in agriculture should have the support and encouragement to do so.

Having discovered my passion and purpose and knowing my *WHY,* many years ago, I also realised I needed to know my *WHAT*. I had to learn to voice to others who asked, exactly what it is that I do.

I posed these questions to myself:
- What can I bring?
- What can I do to help?
- What can we collaborate on?
- What is it that we can do to change the narrative around women and agriculture, in general?

I began to find my national voice through the award I had won and leveraged my passion with food insecurity to talk about it openly. I found other charities I could align with and people who wanted to hear our story. I started to say *YES* to opportunities that found their way into my inbox, phone and meetings through connections.

'I soon realised that recognition and awards matter. In conversations with my male counterparts, I noticed that when they seek speakers, especially women, they look to recognised experts. Understanding this, I actively promote myself and the awards I've won to create connections and opportunities. I self-nominate without hesitation and I consistently nominate other women, ensuring they have the chance to step forward alongside me.'

I uplift others, encouraging them to step in and take over. I don't need to be everything to everyone or always be the face and voice of opportunity. Instead, I value the contributions of others and push them to stop chasing perfection – because success comes from doing what you love with passion and purpose.

Stepping back is just as important as stepping forward. Prioritising self-care and saying *NO* to opportunities that don't align with your values isn't just advisable, it's necessary. I have said *YES* to many things and have been able to sit on boards that pay me, but I don't say *YES* to everything. I do not underestimate this privilege and know that coming from a background of agriculture, loving education and the internal goal of finishing things I start, has led me here and I want as many women as possible to sit alongside me. So, if I decline opportunities, I have more than enough women to nominate to sit in the chair and forge their own path.

This same passion and purpose has led me to career changes and challenges that have opened and closed doors. In May of 2024, I took a risk and went to London, winning a silver in the *Women Changing the World awards for Women in Ag and Farming* – all about food insecurity. I met the Duchess of York and her publisher and felt a connection with her instantly. This has now led me into the world of publishing. I have won a *Gourmand Award* for Best in the World in the Charity and Fundraising Cookbook category. Now, I am leveraging this experience to nurture, publish and promote authors through *Stories that Speak* and KMD Books.

We need to hear more voices and share more stories, whether that be memoirs, non-fiction business insights, cookbooks, children's books or anthologies. I believe in the power of storytelling. Stories inspire, connect and create legacies. Writing, speaking and mentoring are all extensions of the same mission; to amplify voices that need to be heard, elevate experiences that can make a difference and leave a meaningful imprint on the world.

Passion without purpose can be fleeting, but together, they create a force that drives real change. I believe my experiences and choices are a testament to the power of embracing what sets your soul on fire and aligning it with a greater mission. Whether in agriculture, leadership or publishing, my purpose remains the same: to uplift, to advocate and to make a difference … not just for myself, but for the generations that follow.

ABOUT ROBYN

Meet Robyn Verrall, a dynamic force in the world of agriculture. Robyn is not just a successful farmer, she's a passionate leader and a master networker, connecting people and ideas to drive positive change in the community, she is a volunteer, business owner, chair, keynote speaker, winner of numerous awards including being proud co-creator of 'best in the world' Gourmand award-winning cookbook. Her influence extends far and wide, making her a true catalyst for progress of women and girls in the world.

SAOIRSE CONNOLLY
THE VOICE OF MY WOMB

'I feel like I'm numb.' 'I'm so cut off from my creativity.' 'Social media fills me with dread and worry.'

I was feeling so deflated, completely cut off from my passion and purpose. Numb. Disconnected. As if the fire that had once fuelled me had flickered down to embers in my womb. The spark was gone and with it, my certainty, my magnetism, my ability to fully trust in the vision that once pulled me forward with unstoppable precision.

Every time I opened social media, I felt a pang of dread. Doubt crept in like a slow poison, whispering that maybe I wasn't meant to lead, that maybe the world had gone too far and the tipping point was an impossible target to aim for.

It only takes 3.5% of us to initiate radical change in the world through civil disobedience and conscientious resistance and Rebel Ma was my contribution to the revolution. Using the power of story to raise the vibration in service to our collective healing and liberation. But the energy of Rebel Ma, the powerful force driving me forward felt like a distant dream, a story someone else had written.

I had the structure. The strategy. The action plan. But the numbness had crept in. This wasn't a strategic problem. It wasn't a matter of needing a new launch plan or better content. Strategy is only as powerful as the energy it sits on top of. And my energy? It was fractured.

I had forgotten what I knew to be true about feminine leadership.

We are not meant to force or push. We are not meant to hustle our way forward, overriding our own wisdom in pursuit of some external measure of success. Our leadership does not come from checking the right boxes or following some preordained path.

Our power is in the unseen. In the way we allow ourselves to surrender to the mystery. In the way we let ourselves be held, not just by the women around us, but by the ancestors who came before us, the forces moving through us, the great unseen team that is always working in our favour, if only we remember to call them in.

TENDING TO MY WOMB FLAME

I closed my eyes and took a deep breath. I welcomed every feeling; the grief of what we have been collectively witnessing for eighteen months of the most unfathomable, unimaginable, unbearable horror in Palestine. The anger, the helplessness, the doubt, the frustration. I let it all be there. And then, I asked to see what I had been missing. I set aside the belief that I was numb, that my creative channel was blocked. If there was any emotion there, I let it be.

And that's when I could feel them, my ancestors, rallying behind me. All the women who did not have a voice, who were not granted the blessings and protections I had. Those who could not use their magic, who never had access to the tools and technology that now allow us to share our stories with the world. Their wisdom was woven into my DNA, carried through ancestral lines – thousands of powerful women who had made sacrifices for my freedom, standing behind me, breathing life into me.

And there it was, the creative flame in my womb. The fire burning beneath the cauldron of my dreams. It flickered. Like turning the gas on, and it clicked, clicked, clicked … unsure if it wanted to catch like wildfire and explode into something massive, or sputter out because the tank was empty. It was indecisive.

So I bowed before it. I got down on my hands and knees, my feet pressing into the imaginary dirt, and I blew gently on the embers. I called the oxygen in, stoking the tired coals. I had spent the winter season feeling stagnant. But now, as the light began to return, I could feel a thawing. It was time to cultivate the energy, excitement and joy again.

I brought my hands to my womb, our sacred vessel of creativity, passion, purpose, aliveness, femininity. She would burn when she had the fuel. And I was the keeper of that fuel. My beliefs, my actions, my thoughts, they were the offerings I laid upon her fire. So what was I choosing to feed her?

I chose belief. I chose devotion. I chose excitement, motivation, inspiration and trust. I released the pressure to perform. Our creations are entities all of their own. Rebel Ma is unstoppable. She would grow wings and fly, light up lives, activate wombs and liberate women across the skies … when she was ready.

I chose to believe that this was true. That my work mattered. That truth-telling was of the utmost value. That every small act of bravery and creation would activate others to stand up and speak out too.

And that's when the vision came through.

A SANCTUARY WITHIN

A tropical island. Rebel Ma's island. A sanctuary. A portal. A space where women had to choose to cross the threshold, to leave behind the old ways of doing things and enter something deeper, wilder, truer.

I saw them arriving, one by one, in small boats. I saw the nervousness on their faces, the excitement in their eyes. I felt the fire at the center of it all, the fire of our shared purpose, of the stories yet to be told – the sacred fire that has been burning since time immemorial, tended to by the old ancestors long before any of us.

I could feel the energy of the women I was calling into Rebel Ma, where I could tap into the frequency of what we were truly building, not just in the external world, but in the unseen realms where all creation begins. In this island sanctuary, I felt them. The women. The ones who needed me to stop hesitating, stop questioning, stop hiding. They didn't need me to be perfect. They didn't need me to be polished. They didn't need me to be palatable. They needed me to be *in my power*.

And in that moment, everything shifted. I remembered: *I am the guardian of this island. The women who come to me are not here by accident. They have already chosen. They have already signed their soul contracts. My only job is to hold the space, to keep the fire burning, to stand unwavering in my knowing that Rebel Ma is more than a book, she is an act of revolution and a living testament to the return of feminine leadership that is so desperately needed to bring peace, balance and harmony back to the fabric of our society.*

I had spent too much time trying to force my energy out of stagnancy, forgetting we are cyclical beings. We are not meant to be in a constant state of creation, of doing, of producing. That is colonial patriarchal indoctrination. Just as the seasons turn, so too do we. There are times of rapid growth and expansion, but there are also times of stillness, stagnation, even descent.

This can feel frustrating – watching the world burn, feeling the urgency of the work, knowing how much needs to change, while at the same time feeling like inspiration is moving through us at a snail's pace.

The empire is collapsing, and the energy required to resist, defy and dissolve it is massive. Our breaths need to be oceans deep and sky high, the urgency of our mission is undeniable, and yet, there are moments where we feel stuck, where we feel like we can't possibly meet the enormity of what we are here to do.

This is where we must surrender and remember: *stagnation is not failure*. Stagnation is part of the cycle. The void is part of the creation process. Before the rise, there is always a descent. Before expansion, there is contraction.

We descend so that we may rise again and I realised I was bogged down with the weight of needing to save the world but also afraid of promising that a truer, more beautiful world was possible because for a time, I lost my faith in it. I was struggling to believe it, so how could I be an advocate for it?

APOCALYPSE AS REBIRTH: THE PORTAL TO A NEW WORLD

There's no doubt about it, we are living in apocalyptic times. A polycrisis of ecocide, genocide, femicide, the rise of fascism – all threads of the same violent tapestry woven from colonial capitalist white supremacist and patriarchal extraction.

But an apocalypse is not just an end. In ancient mythology, it is the meeting of endings and beginnings, the portal through which a new world can be born.

The root of our severance from our feminine power, from the mother, from the land and from each other, lies in the witch hunts of Europe. Thousands, if not millions, of women, non-binary people and men who lived in radical communion with the Earth, the animals, the ancestors and each other in powerful covens, were murdered by patriarchs who had lost their humanity.

And in the loss of these witches and priestesses, druids and wisdom-keepers who carried the sacred knowledge of the land and lore, the villages lost their soul. With no-one left to carry the knowledge of the Earth and the oracular visions of the ancestors, men were free to build a world of conquest, colonisation and capitalist insanity. We are living inside the consequences of this destruction now.

Yet, the wisdom was never truly lost. It lives in our bones and in our wombs, in the whispers of our grandmothers' prayers on the winds, in the unseen realms waiting for us to remember. We, the modern matriarchs of today, are rising, returning and reimagining the future we want to live in. Walking each other home the new and ancient way. Tapping into the wisdom within that knows what's best for ourselves, our children and all children.

The Rebel Ma Rising movement is here to reawaken the voices of the women who were not allowed to speak. To honour the witches, the healers, the oracles, the medicine women and the rebels in our lineages who were burned, drowned and silenced for daring to stand in their truth.

To liberate the ones who had to swallow their intuition, bury their magic and shrink themselves to survive and to amplify the voices of those who continue to be hunted now in a live streamed genocide right before our eyes – to keep the wisdom stories and traditions alive.

Because let's be honest – the witch hunts never really ended. They just changed form. The same forces that burned our ancestors at the stake are still at work today – just wrapped up in shinier, more socially acceptable PR packaging.

The system is still designed to keep us frozen in apathy or fear, to keep us distracted and divided, stuck in survival. And if we don't rise together in defiance, rooted in revolutionary love, offering up our gifts for the greater good, the ramifications will be far worse for all of us.

It does not matter how we defy and dismantle the predatory systems we are forced to live under, all that matters is that we each find a way to defy them, creatively, humorously, relentlessly and in so doing reclaim some of our lost humanity.

The systems are old. The game is long. They are counting on us to get tired. And there's no denying those of us who are awake and aware can get stuck in our grief, our rage, our shame, our fight, flight or freeze response ... and we sometimes forget the most sacred medicine we carry: *joy*.

HOLD ONTO YOUR JOY

Those of us who stand for liberation – personal and collective – often take ourselves too seriously. We collapse into despair. We forget that joy, laughter and pleasure are not just acts of resistance, they are acts of creation. And in the act of creation, we reclaim our power and agency.

We are each vital to collective liberation. We are women with the ability to conceive, create, gestate and birth life itself. The womb is not just a physical space, she is the seat of our deepest passions, the bridge between worlds, the portal through which spirit becomes form. Our purpose is encoded in her wisdom. We are the midwives of a new world and as women we must listen to the voice of our womb that reminds us we can weave the new world into being with joy and hope and the utmost faith that it's not too late.

Can you hold the grief and the laughter in the same breath? Can you dance through the fire, knowing we are here to help birth something more beautiful? Our children trust us to carry this vision. Let us be worthy of their trust.

Mothers rise even when we are weary, not because it is easy, but because we have a sacred duty. We are the keepers of life, the architects of a new world, the fierce protectors of what must endure.

The world as we know it is collapsing. We stand at the precipice of a rebirth for humanity and no-one is coming to save us. It is we, the people, who are being invited to reclaim our power and learn to walk in right relationship with this Earth and each other.

To remember that all life is sacred. To listen deeply, to recalibrate, to align our bodies, minds and hearts with the rhythms of nature, so that we may ride the waves of this transition rather than be swallowed by them. For we are not just surviving this collapse, we are leading the birth of what comes next.

And we are not just allowed to believe in the possibility of something new – we are required to. Even as empire crumbles, even as the Earth wails, belief is a necessity. It is the frequency of our evolution; the code that unlocks the innate wisdom we need to shape the world we know we deserve.

Our work – building a just, sustainable, liberated world – demands action. But to sustain those actions, we've got to first reclaim our spiritual sovereignty. Because without it, we are playing their game. And we did not come here to be victims of their destruction, we came here to dismantle and be the midwives and matriarchs of creation.

This is why we are here. This is why our existence was prayed into being. This is why we carry the gifts we do, because they are meant to be used. May we remember, may we rise, may we write and may we roar. We are the ones we've been waiting for.

A REBEL MATRIARCH'S ROAR

Mothers know we do not have the luxury of surrendering to despair. We cannot afford to turn away, to shrink, to disappear. We show up, for our children, for their children, for every generation that will follow, because we are the ones who birth the future. We are in the birth canal now. Can you feel it? The pressure, the intensity, the burning transformation? Birth is never easy and neither is revolution. To bring new life forth, a part of us must die. The smallness, the fear, the old patterns of submission, these must be shed so that we may rise as the matriarchs of our tribes and our lives and lead the return to the time of the feminine where life, mothers, children and the Earth come first. This is the prophecy unfolding. Let us not fall into hopelessness. Let us resist oppression, isolation and dehumanisation. Let us choose love over fear. Our medicine is needed now more than ever. We can call upon the strength in our bones, the love in our blood, the resilience of our lineage to fortify our spirits and support us in holding the vision of the world we know is possible for ourselves and our children. A world rooted in regenerative, revolutionary love that refuses to be silent, that prioritises community care and kindness, because this is the call of our times. We are the mothers and midwives of this new world. And we will not be silenced. Hear Us Roar.

ABOUT SAOIRSE

Saoirse Connolly is founder and creatrix of House of Wild Publishing and Rebel Ma Rising - she is leading a movement of modern-day matriarchs reclaiming their voices, rewriting history and alchemising their personal stories into powerful legacies. Saoirse is a two-time international bestselling author and publisher, women's empowerment mentor, international facilitator, voice activator and dream liberator for revolutionary women here to change the world through their soul-led missions. Through her bestselling anthology books, transformative mentorship and rite of passage initiations, Saoirse creates sacred space for women to write, rise & thrive by owning their voices and desires, sharing their truth from a place of power and healing from the inside out to live their most juicy, lit-up and liberated lives. Made in Dublin, Ireland, she now lives in Bali, Indonesia, with her twin flame Darragh and two kids Fiadh and Bodhi. When she's not changing the world, she's travelling it.

Come play on:
Instagram: @sessionswithsaoirse or @rebelmarising
Substack: rebelmarising.substack.com

SAOIRSE CONNOLLY

Website: rebelmarising.com

Or listen to her podcast Rebel Ma presents *All Boobs Blazing for the Feminine Rising* on Apple or Spotify

SCHARRELL JACKSON
THE STRENGTH WITHIN

My journey has been marked by trials, tribulations and a childhood burdened with rejection. At four years old, the words *I never wanted kids anyway* were etched into my heart, creating a wound I carried into adulthood. This rejection left a hole inside me, fuelling a drive for perfection but eroding my confidence and courage. For years, I existed in a space of overachievement, seeking validation in roles and relationships that weren't aligned with who I truly was. I was living for others, not for myself. It took many years and many heartaches to come to terms with the weight that those early words carried, but they shaped my resilience and my determination to keep moving forward.

But something profound began to shift within me when I learned the power of forgiveness – not only toward those who hurt me, but also toward myself. Forgiveness became my doorway to freedom, and with it, I deepened my faith. Faith gave me the clarity to see that every hardship, every disappointment, and every time I felt unseen, were not moments to break me – they were moments to build me. Each of these experiences was like a hammer and chisel, carving out the person I was meant to be.

Often, we mistake trials for failures, but it is in those moments that endurance is truly forged. Endurance isn't just about surviving the storms, it's about thriving through them, and emerging stronger and more determined on the other side. Every hardship I faced became a stone laid in the foundation of who I am today – a woman of endurance, courage and authenticity.

I began to understand that life's difficulties are not the defining moments of our stories, they are merely chapters. The narrative of our lives is ours to rewrite. And so, I made the choice to live with intention, to live worthy of the woman I was created to be.

As an overachiever, I skipped several grades and began working at the age of thirteen. Even at that young age, I found myself constantly over-contributing, overdoing and being the *over-over*, if you know what I mean. Being the eldest child, only eleven months older than my brother, I took on the responsibility of caring for him as if I were a parent. That sense of duty didn't come from any external pressure, it came from my deep need to be validated, to prove I was enough.

I have always been a planner. I had a vision of how my life was supposed to unfold, and in many ways, I was obsessed with achieving it. Getting good grades wasn't just an expectation for me, it became a mission. I sought independence early on, not because I wanted freedom for its own sake, but because I didn't want to be a burden to anyone. I thought that if I could excel, achieve, and surpass expectations, then maybe – just maybe – I would finally feel as if I mattered. By the time I was a young adult, I had climbed to the top of my class and rolled into corporate America, ready to conquer the world.

But life has a funny way of reminding us that success, as we define it early on, doesn't necessarily equate to fulfilment. I had my life planned down to the detail: marry at twenty-three, have my first child by twenty-five, and climb the corporate ladder to achieve the quintessential American Dream. But here's what I learned; *What is a dream if it doesn't fulfil your soul? What good is success if it leaves you empty inside?* I reached the heights I had set out to achieve, but something inside me still felt incomplete.

When I married an incredible man, I thought I had it all. But the truth was, I wasn't whole. I hadn't healed from the wounds of my past and I was still battling demons from poor choices I'd made along the way. I couldn't bring my best self to the table, and neither could my husband. Though he gave his best and loved me deeply, he, too, was unequipped. Our relationship, built on two broken foundations, could only bear so much weight.

There's a common myth that marriage, success or reaching milestones will somehow make us whole. But the truth is, if you enter any partnership (whether it's with a person, a career or even a goal) without first being whole yourself, that foundation is destined to crack. I was living in pieces, torn between my roles as a wife, mother and corporate leader, but never fully stepping into any of them with my full self.

As I navigated my roles as a wife, mother of two and corporate leader, I found myself losing a piece of myself every single day. As an African-American woman in a male-dominated, predominantly white environment, I was constantly shrinking to fit in. On the outside, I wore a badge of success, my life appeared perfect, but on the inside, I was slowly dying.

I wasn't living authentically. I was operating in alignment with what others needed from me, rather than with who I was. I led my organisation with a constant fear of failure, terrified that one misstep would expose me as inadequate. I tried to be the perfect wife, though deep down I hadn't yet embraced my own worth. I raised my children with love, but sometimes I was too hard on them, trying to fill the void that was left by the love I didn't feel I had as a child. Other times, I had no boundaries at all, desperately wanting them to feel loved and validated in ways I never had.

By the time I had climbed the corporate ladder and my marriage was falling apart, I found myself pregnant again. But that pregnancy ended tragically in an ectopic rupture. I remember lying on the hospital bed, surrounded by voices, feeling my life slipping away. In that moment, I made a deal with God. *If you give me one more chance, I promise to live a life in alignment with the gifts you've given me.* I didn't want to be a victim of my circumstance any longer. I no longer wanted to be ruled by my emotions or the expectations of others. I wanted to live as the woman I was born to be.

That near-death experience was a turning point. After the birth of my third child, my marriage eventually ended, but the loss of that child forced me to confront the parts of myself I had been avoiding for years. It was time to stop merely surviving and start truly living. I wanted to live as light.

From that moment on, I became intentional about bringing light into the world. I wanted to heal, to forgive, to let go of the bitterness that had weighed me down for so long. But I quickly realised that healing required endurance; an attribute I would need to cultivate daily. I needed the endurance to forgive, to persevere and to move forward when everything inside me wanted to stay stuck in the past.

Endurance is not just physical, it is mental and spiritual. It is the act of showing up for yourself, even when the weight of the world feels too heavy to carry. Endurance is waking up every day and choosing to keep moving forward. It is making the decision to forgive those who have wronged you, even when the pain still lingers. It is deciding to love yourself, even when the world has told you otherwise.

I stopped focusing on where I had come from and started focusing on where I wanted to go. I was diligent about how I lived my life. I began studying, praying and surrounding myself with a tribe of people who held me accountable. I needed boundaries, not just with others but with myself, so I wouldn't deplete my own cup while pouring into others. I couldn't offer anything of value to the world if I didn't first value myself.

As I grew into this new version of myself, it became less about titles, money and success as defined by the world, and more about living a life of impact and abundance. This is where I found true success, not in the things I had achieved but in the person I had become. Success wasn't about what I owned, but about what I contributed to the world.

I learned the power of prayer, not as a last resort but as a daily practice to open doors I had once thought were locked. I realised that often, we try so hard to force things into being, when in reality, we just need to have the faith to walk through the doors that are already open.

I began to embrace relationships rather than fear them. I stopped sabotaging connections because I believed they were doomed to fail. Instead, I decided to nurture them, to allow others to see me fully and authentically. And through that process, I became the woman I could be proud of – the woman I had been waiting for all along.

This transformation wasn't just for me. I knew that if I could walk this path, others could too. My story wasn't just my own, it was a road map for others to follow. I wanted to show others that even through brokenness, they could find healing. Even in the darkest moments, they could find light.

I had to make peace with my past, to forgive myself for over-extending, over-compensating and over-pleasing. The over-achiever in me was trying to fill the void left by rejection and fear, but I had to realise that no achievement would ever be enough if I didn't believe I was enough. That belief came from the power of faith, from understanding that I didn't need external validation to be worthy. I was born significant … and so are you.

To everyone reading this – your past does not dictate your future. The challenges you've faced are not the end of your story, they are the beginning. Your life is not defined by the struggles you've endured but by the choices you make moving forward. Choose to live with endurance, to persevere through difficulty and to embrace the attributes that make you uniquely powerful.

You are not the sum of your setbacks. You are the author of your future. And the ending of your story is yours to write.

It's important to understand that endurance is not a one-time act.

It is the daily, consistent decision to rise, to face your fears, to confront your obstacles with courage and resilience. It means having the faith to walk through doors when you cannot see what's on the other side. It means making peace with your past, not erasing it, but embracing it as the foundation of who you are and what you've learned.

But endurance also demands restoration. You cannot pour from an empty cup. One of the most profound lessons I've learned is that rest and recovery are as much a part of endurance as persistence. It's about knowing when to push forward, and when to step back, refuel and allow yourself the grace of healing. Often, we think of endurance as relentless, never stopping, but true endurance requires the wisdom to pause, to assess and to rejuvenate when necessary. This is not weakness – it is wisdom.

Endurance also calls for boundaries. For so long, I didn't know how to say no. I equated worth with how much I could give, how much I could endure, how much I could achieve for others. But true endurance is also the courage to say yes to yourself. It is the understanding that you are your greatest investment and that nurturing yourself – your mind, body and spirit – is non-negotiable. Boundaries are not walls to shut people out, they are the gates through which you let love, respect and abundance flow in and out of your life.

Courage, similarly, is not the absence of fear. Courage is acting in spite of fear. It is stepping into spaces that are uncomfortable, challenging and unknown, not because you are fearless, but because your desire to grow is greater than your fear of failing. Every courageous step I've taken in my life was accompanied by fear, but I have learned that fear is just a part of the journey. It's not an enemy to be conquered, but a companion to be acknowledged and moved through. Let fear have a voice, but never let it have a vote in your decisions.

Resilience is born from these courageous acts. It is the ability to rise each time you fall, knowing every setback is not an ending, but an invitation to try again – smarter, stronger and wiser. Resilience is not about avoiding the fall, it's about bouncing back with even more determination and grace. It is learning how to pivot when your plans don't work out and to trust that even when life doesn't go as planned, you are still on the path to your purpose.

Living authentically, for me, has been the most liberating and profound step in this journey. For years, I wore masks; masks of perfection, masks of success, masks of *being enough*. But authenticity is the shedding of those masks. It's standing in the full truth of who you are; your flaws, your strengths, your insecurities and your brilliance. It's allowing yourself to be seen, fully, and not shrinking to make others comfortable.

Authenticity is freedom. It is living in alignment with who you were created to be, not who the world tells you to be. It's being bold enough to say, *This is me*, and to know that your worth is not contingent upon external validation. The moment I started living authentically, I realised I was no longer chasing approval. I had finally become comfortable in my own skin, and that confidence became magnetic. I started attracting people, opportunities and experiences that aligned with my true self.

I want you to remember that you are already enough. You were enough the moment you were born, and you will continue to be enough, no matter what you face. Life will try to tell you otherwise, and circumstances may challenge your belief in your worth, but your value is intrinsic. You do not need to earn it. You need only to believe it.

Because beyond every setback is a greater comeback. Beyond every heartache is healing. And beyond every challenge, is a version of yourself waiting to roar with power, grace and authenticity.

The life you desire is within your reach … if only you have the courage to reach for it.

ABOUT SCHARRELL

Scharrell Jackson is a distinguished international keynote speaker, global executive coach, and celebrated author with over twenty-five years of executive leadership experience. She has earned multiple prestigious honors, including the 2025 Women Changing the World Global Coach of the Year Award, Gender Diversity Award and Diversity, Inclusion and Belonging Award, Orange County Business Woman of the Year, AICPA's Most Powerful Woman in Accounting Award, and the NAWBO Remarkable Woman Award to name a few. Renowned for her transformative impact as a partner and chief operations, financial and administrative officer, she has driven 25% year-over-year growth, scaled revenues from $3.5M to $400M, achieved 95% staff retention, and reduced operational expenses by over 25%, creating operational efficiency and building nationally recognized great place to work culture.

As the CEO of STJ Consulting Services, she empowers leaders through her highperformance coaching and keynote speaking to rise above and achieve unparalleled success. Scharrell is a top-ranked executive coach with over 40,000+ hours working with C-Suite leaders and the architect of the proprietary "Endgame Excellence" methodology, a transformative framework designed for ambitious, accomplished leaders ready to elevate from success to significance. Her approach guides leaders in making precise, outcome-driven decisions, ensuring sustained high performance and remarkable clarity to strategically navigate the complexities of leadership that solidify their legacy.

As a captivating international speaker, Scharrell electrifies audiences with keynotes on transformative leadership, operational excellence, and high-impact decisionmaking. With over a decade of speaking engagements, her signature keynote, "*The Power of Decision*," empowers leaders to make strategic choices with boldness and clarity. Her celebrated *High-Performance Leadership* series also features "The Impact on the Bottom Line," exploring how vision, leadership, performance, and strategy converge to drive organizational success. Sought-after topics such as *Conquering Imposter Syndrome* and *Self-Care: The Best Version of You* resonate deeply with professionals dedicated to authentic, balanced leadership. Scharrell's work redefines how leaders navigate challenges, empowering them to take decisive, transformative action. Her Mandate is **HIGH-PERFORMANCE LEADERSHIP**, and her promise is **DECISIVE EXCELLENCE**.

SHELEILA D'PAIVA
EMPOWERING WOMEN, ONE STEP AT A TIME

I've always had a restless energy inside me, an urge to create, to help, to lead and most importantly, to empower. Maybe it's the Capricorn in me; grounded and driven, with a deep sense of responsibility to build something meaningful. Maybe it's my human design – manifestor 1/3, the initiator, the trailblazer, the one who feels the pull to start new things, to create, to push boundaries. Maybe, because my life path is thirty-three – to be a guide and a source of inspiration for others. Or maybe it's the fact that I've spent my life navigating and shaping who I am out of what was handed to me, including the complexities of growing up around family violence and experiencing my mother raise three children alone. Whatever the reason, it's my *why* that's shaped my journey, and it's the compass I follow every day.

I often reflect on the various chapters of my life. I'm the proud owner of a commercial cleaning business, the co-owner of a finance broking firm, an international award-winning author, an artist and a passionate board member and treasurer for Consumers of Mental Health WA (CoMHWA). Each of these roles may seem distinct, yet they're all tied together by one central thread; empowering women and making a positive impact on the world around me.

When I look at what I do, it feels like the universe is constantly calling me to test my limits and explore new possibilities. I didn't start out with a road map. I had to stumble along the way, trying things out, failing, learning and growing from it all. It's been a dance of trial and error, but I wouldn't have it any other way. I embrace the journey with all its twists and turns, and through it, I always find passion and purpose.

Growing up in a household shaped by family violence was a defining experience for me. I have vivid memories of the day we ran away, and my mum struggling financially as we grew up, a memory of being given rations of water to shower only surfacing recently. She embedded a deep sense of resilience within me as I watched her manage the household and give us everything we needed to get by. Whilst it came with its own fear of scarcity, it taught me early on how crucial it is to build a life on my own terms; one of independence, security and high self-worth. It also taught me the importance of empathy and compassion for others, especially women who find themselves in toxic environments and have seemingly limited options.

Yet, there were beautiful memories amidst the dark ones too as I watched my mum flourish. After migrating to Australia, she was unable to continue teaching English due to the differing education systems, so she became a travel agent. She also delved into the world of led lighting, network marketing, vending machines and ultimately re-married, worked FIFO and built a multimillion-dollar property portfolio with her now-husband. She never sat still and she never allowed herself to wallow in her circumstance – she couldn't with the three of us counting on her. It wasn't through her words, but through her actions, that she taught me one of the most powerful lessons of my life: we can try anything we want. There is no such thing as failure, only learning. And, we have the ability to change the course of our lives – lessons I wouldn't fully understand until my later adult years.

This is why I started writing, to try it, to express myself. My first book wasn't meant to be published. It was something for myself, something I imagined handing down to my kids one day, a story they could pass on to theirs. But on a whim, I ordered one hundred copies and decided to sell them at The Every Woman Expo, a three-day event. I set up a fold-out table with a white tablecloth I didn't even iron, feeling absolutely ridiculous for putting myself out there like that. And yet, to my surprise, I sold them all. More than that, I connected with so many women who later reached out and shared how much they resonated with the story. That experience sparked something in me, a desire to write more, to connect through words.

From there, I wrote a children's book, *The Quacking Frog*, then contributed to anthologies like *The FIFO Wives' Tales* and *Love, Bruises & Bullshit*, where I shared deeply personal experiences. Seven years after that initial book launch, I rewrote the original novel and published it as *Dancing Skies & City Lights*. It was just as successful as the first and I realised how much my writing reflected my desire to connect with others.

Dancing Skies & City Lights is a novel that explores the journeys we take based on the decisions we make, the people we meet and the serendipitous moments that change the course of our lives. But beneath the adventure and travel that Katie, the protagonist, begins to pursue, there's a deeper message – a reminder that we can find ourselves in unexpected places and that it's never too late to take a new path.

My latest novel, and the sequel, *Sacred Minds & Sunlit Souls*, explores the complexities of life, love and further self-discovery. Katie continues to question where she's at and begins to make decisions based on how she wants her future to look. Along the way, she encounters characters who challenge her, and in doing so, she takes meaningful steps toward the future she desires. It's a story close to my heart because it delves into psychology, manifestation and values-driven decision-making, which is something that has changed my life.

It was during these pivotal learnings for myself I started my finance broking business with an old colleague of mine – *ICS Business & Finance*. It was a time during a redundancy when I had nearly run out of money and was considering selling one of my properties to get by. I had applied for fifty jobs and been on thirty-seven interviews/calls/catch ups and coffees and still hadn't been offered anything. I was either over-qualified or under-qualified for the roles available, and I decided I wouldn't allow myself to be in that position again. While one of the darkest times in my life, it was also a blessing in disguise.

My now business partner called me and asked if I wanted to start a finance broking business with her. That night, I sent her the business plan that had been sitting on my laptop for months. I had always wanted to start my own business, but was scared of taking the leap without having a consistent flow of income. She loved it. And the rest is history. Our business supports people purchasing their first home, investment properties, equipment for their personal life or business and commercial loans for business expansion and acquisitions. While I talk numbers a lot, it's not just about money for me, it's about creating opportunities for individuals and entrepreneurs. It's about financial empowerment, particularly for those who might not have the knowledge or resources to navigate it alone. I believe in the power of finance to transform lives and, when I work with individuals or businesses, I see it as a chance to make a broader impact. I look forward to being able to help disadvantaged women with financial literacy through this vehicle in the future as well.

This drive for empowerment is also why my commercial cleaning business, Aspira Cleaning, is more than just a business to me. It's a platform for change. I don't just want to offer cleaning services, I want to elevate the cleaning industry by ensuring my employees receive fair wages and respect. Cleaning is often a profession that is overlooked and undervalued, yet it's the only vehicle for many to receive income and I see the potential of this industry to be so much more. I'm proud to offer opportunities for women, particularly those leaving domestic violence relationships, to rebuild their lives with confidence and financial independence. Through this business, I aim to create an environment where people feel empowered, supported and valued.

Weaved between working full-time (at the time), writing or business endeavours, I also took the steps to learn how to paint. First, I had to draw, week by week, building my skill set. Once I had mastered this, my mentor allowed me to progress to painting. Even my paintings uncovered my natural pull toward diversity and empowerment; painting women, cultures or the human form. It's what I love. Reflecting back, I feel this experience was less about the paint and more about the personal challenge; to grow, to stretch myself, to focus, to try something new, to struggle, to be patient with progress, to be in awe of art, and then, to have my paintings accepted into local art awards.

In all of this – finance, cleaning, writing, art – there is a common thread. It's about not succumbing to our own limiting beliefs. It's about breaking barriers and helping people rise above their circumstances. It's about finding strength in vulnerability and finding purpose in the things that matter most.

Being on the board of Consumers of Mental Health WA (CoMHWA), where I also serve as treasurer, is an extension of my commitment to making a difference. The organisation's work in the mental health advocacy space is something I deeply resonate with. Mental health, much like financial independence, is a critical part of living a fulfilling life. Through CoMHWA, I've had the privilege of working with others who teach me so much, sharing the same passion for advocacy and giving back – it's been incredibly rewarding. I believe in the importance of community and creating space for people to feel seen and supported.

I often feel that I'm called to lead, not in the traditional sense, but in a way that encourages others to step into their power. It's not always easy. There are moments of imposter syndrome, moments of doubt, but when I look at the work I'm doing, the lives I'm touching and the difference I'm making, I know I'm on the right path.

So, what drives me? What's the real fuel behind everything I do? It's simple. It's my desire to empower people, especially women who've faced adversity or discrimination.

It's my urge to give back and make this world a little better then how I found it, to make sure that every person who walks through my doors, whether in my cleaning business or my finance practice, feels valued, supported and resilient. It's my need to embrace new challenges, to try new things and to constantly grow. Every role I take on, every venture I pursue, is a step closer to the world I want to create; a world where women can thrive, break free from limiting circumstances and become the best versions of themselves.

I once heard the phrase, *'You can't be what you can't see,'* and it stuck with me. It's part of why I do what I do. I want to be visible, so that other women, especially women of colour who have faced adversity, can see what's possible for them. I want to show them they can rise, they can build, they can lead. That no matter where they start, they can create the life they deserve.

I don't have it all figured out, and I'm okay with that. I know that each step I take, each project I embark on, is part of the bigger picture … and I can only see so far. I have learned to trust that what's meant for me, will come. As I continue to walk this path, I'll do it with the same passion, dedication and heart that I've put into everything else. Because this journey isn't just about me – it's about everyone I get to empower along the way.

ABOUT SHELEILA

Sheleila D'Paiva is a passionate finance broker, entrepreneur, writer, artist and community advocate dedicated to empowering others and making a positive impact. She is also a 2025 Australian Business Elite 40 Under 40 Winner.

With a background in accounting, banking and finance, she specialises in commercial lending, helping small-to-medium businesses navigate financial challenges and grow. Her work ensures that entrepreneurs have the financial tools they need to succeed and focuses on supporting women with financial literacy.

In addition to her finance career, Sheleila is the founder of Aspira Cleaning, a commercial cleaning business with a strong social mission. Aspira not only provides high-quality cleaning services but also offers job opportunities for women who have experienced domestic violence. Sheleila's personal experiences growing up in a family affected by violence have shaped her commitment to helping vulnerable women regain their independence and rebuild their lives through employment.

Sheleila has multiple books – from novels, a children's book and chapters in multiple anthologies sharing her non-fictional personal experiences. Her books explore themes of self-discovery, travel and personal transformation, resonating with readers who enjoy stories of growth and connection.

Beyond her professional ventures, Sheleila is actively involved in mental health advocacy as a board member of CoMHWA, where she serves as treasurer. Her passion for giving back to the community is central to everything she does.

Whether helping businesses thrive, empowering women in need or telling meaningful stories through her writing, Sheleila D'Paiva is driven by a desire to uplift others and create lasting change.

VAL QUINN
BARCELONA FULL IRONMAN

SWIM 900M/14:13; BIKE 180KM/8:01;

RUN 42.2KM/5:15

My triathlon journey started in early 2019, with a sprint triathlon in Donegal – and what a journey it has been. I decided then that I wanted to get fit and lose some weight, so landed on Dunlaoire half ironman (IM) Aug 2019 as an ideal goal, given I was born and bred there. I joined Piranha Tri club as a friend of mine was a member and spoke so highly of the club and the friends she had made there. At the time, I was working a global job, so fitting in the training for the challenge was tough, given I was travelling out of the country four days a week. It meant swimming in some interesting places abroad, like historic baths in Berlin. When I started with the Dunlaoire training, I decided to sign up for the full Ironman in Barcelona for 2020, as I figured I couldn't just do a HALF of something – I need to aim for a FULL.

Dunlaoire race happened in August 2019, and I had a great race. Everything went to plan, as trained and prepared for and I really enjoyed it, despite Dunlaoire half IM claiming to be in the top three most difficult half IM competitions, due to the very tough cycle into the mountains, with the first 50km of the bike ride being uphill!

Buoyed by the Dunlaoire experience, and post a few months light training, the full IM training started in earnest in February 2020.

Covid struck and thus, a couple of months in, it became evident that the IM Barcelona was at risk and, by mid-summer, it was cancelled. So, I continued with only some light training for the rest of the year. Barcelona 2021 (which is actually held one hour outside Barcelona, in a small town called Calella) was announced for 3 October 2021 and real training began again at the start of March 2021. For the first few months, we all weren't sure if the race would even happen in 2021, given the Covid situation, but by mid-summer, we believed it would, so I started to take the training a little more seriously. So I hooked up with three friends from my triathlon club for their long Sunday cycles, for which they liked to get up early on a Sunday to get them done and dusted by lunch. That usually meant a 6:30am start for me to be ready and get to meet them and cycle around Rush and Slane.

The end of September came around quickly and before we knew it, we were flying to Barcelona with a bag packed like I've never packed before – given all the triathlon paraphernalia that's required. I was delighted to have great support with family and friends coming to Barcelona and lots of others downloading the app in anticipation of tracking my progress. No pressure!

I became an avid follower of the Calella weather for the week before I travelled (though friends would say I constantly look at the weather reports no matter where I am!), and it seemed that the Calella weather was going to be very changeable. We arrived Wednesday night before the planned race on Sunday, figuring it would allow plenty of time to settle in and test the bike on a little bit of the course. I'd had a lot of trouble with my rear wheel for a few weeks before departure, with several visits to the bike shop, and it finally being fixed on my third tubeless tyre, with plenty of sealant. We did a short spin on Thursday, which resulted with a small shard of glass in my front tyre, which I gingerly removed and filled with superglue. Given that, and as all seemed okay, I decided I wouldn't touch the bike again until race day.

Thursday night my back was a little sore and by the time I woke on Friday morning, I could hardly get out of bed; my back had seized and I struggled to walk. Luckily, mum is a retired physio and gave me some exercises and stretches to do. In addition, Spain is great for over-the-counter medication without prescription, so I had a few visits to the farmacia for those. A chiropractor friend flew in late Friday. As she manipulated and cracked my back on Saturday, we all felt I could at least make the start line – phew!

On the evening before the race, we had an early dinner. Nerves didn't seem too bad all round and we went to bed early, but I didn't sleep well — with race anticipation, I got about five hours in total. Rising at 5:15am, I did some back stretches and had breakfast, followed by a 2km walk with wetsuit in hand, to the bike area to put the 'nutrition' on the bike at 7:15am, to be ready for the swim gathering at 8:15am.

The weather had turned nasty overnight and there were 29km/hr winds with terrible gusts. The half IM was due to start before us at 8am. The announcer said that everything was being pushed back by thirty minutes, and shortly after that announced that the swim was being shortened for the half and full IM to 900m, due to the winds, large waves and very strong currents. The sea was *mad* looking. Our time came and we started to move forward towards the sea. We could see that the elites had started and were all over the place, many missing the first buoy. The safety kayaks were being overturned and even the man on the safety jet ski fell off! On we marched on the sand, towards the sea and our destiny.

I had a lucky water entry, somehow timing a wave and ducking in with ease. Others were not so lucky, many tried to enter the water but were abruptly spat out by the power of the sea and put right back onto the beach. At this point, some decided their race was over for the day, left questioning their IM journey. Another brave soul wanted to get in, so asked the marshalls for help. One took his arms and another took his legs, and together they swung him twice, throwing him past the large wave breaking on the shore. Now that is SOME WAY to start the swim course!

Our swim challenge was now 900m in extremely rough sea, with waves as high as a one-storey building. I tried to time it so I could sight the buoy when I was on the crest of the wave. As I came down the other side, other swimmers would fall on top of me and I would push them off quickly. However mad it sounds, it was actually quite good fun riding the Calella sea roller-coaster. At last, the big red IM triangle buoy was reached with lots of people flailing around it. Rounding the bend, I sighted the IM arch and headed for land. The strong current, now with us, made the swim fast and furious. A few meters to the beach our exit being the steep stoney incline, saw many IM volunteers bravely waiting with outstretched arms to help pull us out. I looked up and saw an outstretched arm and was trying to grab it when I saw the facial expression of the arm-owner suddenly change (I wish I'd had a camera to capture the moment). Suddenly a huge wave crashed on my head, I tumbled and was pulled back out to sea, with many other competitors tumbling around me and into me; a washing machine experience. I found daylight again, gasped for air, threw myself at another outstretched arm and made it out of the water on the second attempt. Normally on a swim exit, we would start to pull off our hat and goggles and pull the wetsuit to waist level, but everyone seemed a little dazed and none of that started until into the transition (T1) area.

T1 was chaotic with people given the short swim, so I was pleased to get out of there in about nine minutes and onto the bike. Barcelona IM is generally considered a good 'first' full IM as the bike course has a reputation for being relatively flat and fast. Personally, I wouldn't say flat exactly! There is a steady incline for about the first 50km and with the extremely strong headwinds, the bike was feeling tough, sapping my energy. I was trying to find my pace without receiving a penalty for drafting. We reached 36km, where there was a turn and relief from the wind for a few kilometers. As we turned, I heard the person behind me saying, 'Thank f*** for that!' which did make me smile.

At 60km, I suddenly started to feel the bike slide a little. I looked down and realised my back tyre was extremely soft. I had two gas cylinders in my seat bag and decided to stop and try to give it a blast and inflate it, hoping the tubeless sealant would seal any damage with the pressure. I stopped and screwed the cylinder gadget in, but it didn't work. So I unscrewed it, screwed it again and gave the tyre a blast. This time it worked, but it went all over my shoe and put no air into the tyre! My option at this point was to remove the wheel, then the tyre and try to fit a tube to the tubeless tyre, hoping the one remaining gas cylinder would work; if it didn't work I would have no wheel and my IM race would be over. I decided this was too risky an option to take, and decided to keep going on the now very soft back wheel. I cycled to the 85km mark where there was a 'mechanico' and pulled in. He was busy relaxing, listening to music and eating an Iberica ham bocadillo. I energetically asked him if he could help me remove the tyre and put in the spare tube I had in my bag. He spoke little English, declined and pointed to a bike pump a few meters away. I quickly pumped the tyre and cycled on. I reached the 90km turnaround, and by the time I had got back to the 'mechanico' station at 95km again, I stopped again to use Mr Bocadillo's pump. He told me there was another 'mechanico' 50km on and I planned to stop there too. The tyre rapidly deflated again, so with that 50km under my belt, I shouted at an IM steward at the roundabout 'mechanico … mechanic … mechanic …' He shrugged … and that was that. I couldn't see nor find the next 'mechanic'. I pushed on. At this stage, I was being passed constantly by other competitors and the course was starting to be a lonely place. There was no danger of receiving a drafting penalty anymore.

I had stuck to my nutrition plan but by 120km, my stomach was cramping badly. I had worn two bike shorts and a cycle top I had tried in training, issue free (nothing new on race day!). But for some reason today, the shorts bands were digging into me and I was cramping badly, probably not helped by the extra effort to cycle with a flat back tyre into gale force headwinds. I started to feel really unwell. Suddenly at the 120km mark, I began vomiting. In fact, four projectile vomits – I could have scored points for distance and sound! I vomited nearly the equivalent of the 4 x 750ml bottles of nutrition I had consumed to that point – better out than in perhaps!

The bike now had a fully flat back tyre and I was still cramping, but not as badly. I saw, on the other side of the road, the sweeper truck with one bike on the back. *Dammit, he is now so close ... push, push, push, Val ... up the pace so as not to get caught by the truck and be removed from the race.* 20km to go and alone on the road, a white van slowed and pulled up alongside me. The front passenger looked at me, pointing to the rear tyre, saying 'Boom! Boom!' He had no English but was informing me I had a flat rear wheel! He pointed to the roadside gesturing help, but I told him I only had 20km to go now and didn't have time to stop. At this point, the sweeper truck was looming in my mind. Not that he really understood all that, but he smiled with a thumbs up and drove off as fast as he'd arrived.

It had started to rain a little and the ground was wet. At last, I reached Calella, racing downhill around the big roundabout and down towards the sea. I saw my family and friends excitedly and eagerly shouting, smiling and waving, with phones out taking pictures and a video of my arrival. I slowed a lot to take the turn, but before I knew it, given the flat tyre and riding on the rim, the bike had gone from under me and I was separated from the bike, as we both slid along the wet ground with my water bottles flying!

My supporters' faces went from happily smiling and shouting, to ones of fear and worry! I seemed to bounce and found my feet as fast I had lost them, stood up, grabbed my bike, waved to them, shook myself a little and remounted. 1.5km to go which I did at snail's pace to ensure no further falls, given the back wheel rim on the wet roads. I arrived into transition (T2) 8hrs and 1min after I'd left; an exhausting cycle which should have taken me 6.5-7 hrs, but happy to be off the bike at last. I changed quickly and headed out to the run course, thankful that the fall hadn't reactivated my back issue and that I was able to walk. My plan for the run was to run the first 5km at an average pace of 6:15/km and then slower for the next 10km and after 15km probably walk/run. (I'd had some knee issues for the six weeks pre-race with weekly physio to try to sort that and get me to the start line. Due to this, the longest run I'd done in training, pre-race was 22km.)

Well, nothing about the day had gone to plan and the run was no different. At the start, I could hardly walk as my stomach was cramping again. I mostly walked the first 3km and decided to take no nutrition onboard and just drink the water and Cola that was being offered at the drinks stations … at least until I might start to feel better again. About 4km in, I started to feel okay and started to run and then run/walk for most of the way. As the water and cola was working, I took no other nutrition.

At the halfway mark, I stopped for my special needs bag, in which I had a packet of Tayto Salt n Vinegar crisps. That was the best piece of advice I ever got – a delicious treat and plenty of salt to help me along. I continued to run/walk … run/walk … run/walk … – not a bad strategy giving me an average pace of 7:35m/km for most of the course.

The run course is a very flat three loops which means it's excellent for supporters to see you many times. Wow – what an experience … and I loved it … All the supporters look at your race name and number and shout encouragement, all clapping. I was delighted to see my family and friends many times, which truly spurred me on and gave me the belief and encouragement I needed. A BIG THANK YOU to them all. Also, I knew a lot of friends and family at home were tracking my progress, which was a big incentive to keep going, so a big thanks to them also.

I was on the last leg of my last loop, when I suddenly saw my brother. He shouted at me, 'The cut-off time has been shortened, you need to pick up the pace. You have fifteen minutes.' I had approximately 2.5km still to go. My average pace had slowed to just over eight minutes and now I was faced with 2.5km in fifteen minutes! That meant, run the last section at a pace of under 6min/km! I couldn't believe it! I couldn't imagine failing at the last hurdle. I started to sprint as fast as I could, tracking about 5:50m/km for those last very hard 2.5km.

I rounded the last bend to join the red carpet and knew I was home. I'd nearly given myself a heart attack in those last few kilometers … but I'd done it! I slowly jogged the red carpet to suck up the amazing atmosphere, and wave at my family and friends, to hear those infamous words, at last, 'Val Quinn, you are an IRONMAN!' What we didn't find out until later, was that the cut-off time hadn't been shortened – the announcer had got it wrong!

ABOUT VAL

Val Quinn, a Dublin, Ireland, native, earned an honours bachelor of commerce (BComm) degree from University College Dublin (UCD) in 1989. Following this, she obtained a Master in Business Studies (marketing) the subsequent year. In the early 1990s, amidst Ireland's recession, Val, like many others, moved to London, accumulating four years of experience in sales and marketing, before returning home to work for Baileys Irish Cream, Mars Masterfoods and a seventeen-year career with The Coca-Cola Company.

Since departing The Coca-Cola Company in 2021, Val has launched her own business, Tilly (tilly.ie), serving as a business trainer, executive and life coach. Through her work, Val is passionate about inspiring people to lead purpose-driven lives. She encourages self-reflection and proactive steps, advocating for intentional choices that can lead to a more fulfilling and purposeful life aligned with one's aspirations.

VIKKI SPELLER
YOU ARE THE PURPOSE
FOLLOW THE WHISPERS OF YOUR SOUL

There comes a point in many of our lives where a quiet question begins to echo in the background; *What am I really here for?* We might be doing all the things we thought we were supposed to do, we might even be ticking boxes and kicking goals, and yet something feels flat. As if we're going through the motions, smiling on the outside while wondering, on the inside, where the spark went.

You're not alone in that feeling.

As a Holistic Counsellor, Meditation and Mindfulness Coach, and Circle Facilitator for nearly two decades, I've had the honour of sitting in sacred spaces with women, listening, guiding and holding space … and I've learned that this question is more common than we often admit. And while each story is unique, there's a common thread I hear over and over again; "I just don't know what my purpose is." Or "I used to feel passionate about things but now I just feel stuck." Or sometimes "I know what I want but I don't know how to bring it into reality."

Whether you're at the beginning of that questioning, or deep in the search, I want you to know this; *you are not broken.* You are not behind. You haven't missed your moment.

For many, the idea of purpose has to be some grand, impactful mission. There is pressure to know it, name it and live it. That if we haven't figured it out or we're not changing lives on a global scale, then we must be failing. But here's what I've come to know deeply, your purpose does not have to be some grand achievement. I believe our greatest purpose is something far more grounded ... and deeply human.

Our purpose is to *be*. To live. To experience. To learn. To grow. To love and be loved. To share kindness even in small and quite ways. To follow what lights us up. To laugh with our whole being. To cry when we need to. To rest without guilt. To create without pressure. To show up as ourselves ... fully and completely.

Our purpose can be as simple and profound as living each day with intention, kindness and presence. It can be choosing joy, even when life feels heavy. It can be showing up for yourself and others with love.

Purpose isn't always a job title or a role for which there is so much pressure placed upon us in society. Sometimes, it's simply in how we touch the lives of those closest to us. It might be being the most present parent we can be, raising your children with patience and compassion. Or nurturing an idea that's been sitting within your heart for years. Or becoming a more peaceful version of yourself, each day by choosing to forgive, to grow, to speak your truth and heal. Your purpose may be to simply experience life in all its layers, the beautiful, the messy and the unexpected, allowing yourself to keep showing up with an open heart.

I truly believe that every single one of us is born with purpose. And while it may not look the same for you as it does for me or someone else, that's a wonderful thing! Because each of our paths are unique to us.

What I've noticed over the years, is that many women get stuck in the *not knowing*, sitting with me and stating, "But I don't know what lights me up!" overthinking what brings them joy. And I understand, as many of us have spent so much of our lives caring for others, and meeting expectations placed upon by ourselves and others. Or we're living in survival mode, so haven't allowed ourselves the space to let the answers be felt or heard. Most seem to be waiting for a lightning bolt moment to show them the way, so they have no doubt as to what their purpose is.

But what if it's not about that one big defining moment in your life? What if your purpose has already been guiding you through *small things*? The conversation you held where you made someone feel seen. That creative spark that you keep telling yourself, *you'll do one day*. Or that quiet inner-knowing that something is meant for you, even if it doesn't make perfect sense yet. These aren't coincidences, they are breadcrumbs leading you back to yourself. To what fuels your spirit.

So, what is it that stops us from following our purpose? One of the things that often blocks us from discovering or embracing our purpose is *fear*, which can show up through many different beliefs, fear of judgment, fear of failure or even fear of success. Fear that we are not good enough, ready enough or worthy of more. The list is endless and different for everyone depending on their life experiences. I've also sat with women who knew exactly what they wanted to do but were frozen by the idea of doing it, holding their dreams and passions back behind layers of self-doubt and uncertainty.

But I also believe that what lights us up is not random either: that's passion - and passion is our compass. That inner pull you feel, that sense of excitement when you talk about something or do something that fills your cup, this is your soul speaking, guiding you along your path. It's what leads you, the gentle nudge, the whisper of your soul, the thing that makes time disappear when you do it. Passion is the spark that leads you to your purpose and when you follow what sparks joy, even in small ways, you begin to align with who you really are.

When life feels like it flows, that's alignment - not meaning that everything is perfect but there's an ease, a sense of peace. A knowing that you're moving in the direction that feels right for you. Throughout my life, if I have ever felt out of alignment with the flow of life or been unsure of which direction to take, I sit in stillness. Sometimes we just need to quiet the noise. And within the stillness, we allow ourselves to release the noise of comparison, of outside opinions, of the endless to-do-lists and the internal dialogue that tells us we should be further ahead. Purpose often reveals itself when we come back to ourselves and allow ourselves to be still enough to listen. When we dare to believe that joy is a worthy compass. I feel, for many, that it's less about *finding* your purpose and more about *remembering* it.

I believe that one our greatest purposes is to live in the present. As a mindfulness teacher, I see again and again how the magic happens in the moment. When we're grounded and connected, we're able to feel what's true for us. We stop running. We listen. We soften. We begin to understand that being here, being alive, is already a gift.

And it's in that presence we start to reconnect with what truly matters. With what feels natural. That's where purpose is born; it's from within, not from pressure of the outside world. The way we move through life, our energy, our presence, our words, all create a ripple effect. And while we don't always see firsthand the impact, it doesn't mean it isn't there. You may never know the full extent of how your kindness, creativity or honesty has quietly helped someone else - *it all matters*.

Many of the women I work with feel they have lost their passion. They're tired and have given so much to others, whether that be their partners, children, careers or responsibilities. They've forgotten what it feels like to be lit up from the inside, so they wait for clarity, or time to pass or for permission from others, or for something to change in their lives. And this is where I help women return to themselves, as they have peel back the layers and reconnect with their inner-knowing. This is my passion; this is my purpose.

And I've found, that it's often in the simplest of practices that the most powerful shifts happen. I invite you to give yourself permission to explore. As I often share with women in my circles, you don't have to have it all figured out to be on the right path. Your path can unfold step by step, breath by breath. You just need to be willing to listen and allow yourself to pause, feel and trust what you discover along the way.

What if you could just take one gentle step today, allowing yourself the space to do something that ignites your soul? Or what if you simply became curious about what brings you joy, about what fills your energy or what feels *true* for you?

If you are feeling lost or unsure about your purpose or what lights you up, know that you are not alone. And know that there are ways to begin exploring your purpose, right here and now. You are not broken, nor behind. You are unfolding.

I want to offer you three gentle tools that may help you with your passion and purpose and most importantly with yourself.

THREE GENTLE TOOLS TO REIGNITE YOUR PASSION AND DISCOVER PURPOSE

1. Journaling to Find Joy

I want to invite you into a short journaling practice by taking a moment to go inward, gently without pressure. If you're unsure about your passion or what lights you up, this is a beautiful place to begin.

Find a quiet space and take a few slow breaths and drop into your heart. Then allow yourself to explore these journal prompts.

- When was the last time I felt truly alive?
- What did I love doing as a child that I haven't done in years?
- When in my life do I lose track of time because I'm enjoying myself so much?
- If I could spend a day doing anything, just for me, what would that look like?

Write freely and let the whispers of your heart speak. Your purpose can be hidden within the things that bring us joy. (For more journal prompts see link in Bio)

2. Mindful Energy Check-In

One thing I've learned over the years is that purpose isn't something we chase, it's something we tune into. And one of the most helpful ways we can do that, is by creating space to hear ourselves and becoming aware of our energy.

Pause at the end of each day, close your eyes and reflect. Feel your breath. With each breath out, release any pressure to *figure anything out*. Simply breath. Notice. Be. This tiny pause helps reduce the noise so you can start to hear your own rhythm again. The more we practice stillness, the more we reconnect with what's real for us.

When you feel ready ask yourself:
- What gave me energy today?
- What drained me or felt out of alignment?
- Where did I say *yes* when I really meant *no*?
- What's one gentle shift I could make tomorrow to support myself better?

When you do this simple practice regularly, you'll start to notice patterns. Certain people, places or tasks either energise you or pull you down. This exercise will help to bring awareness, which then creates spaces for alignment. Gently start to take steps towards what lights you up.

3. The Soul Spark List

Here's something I love to share when women tell me they're stuck or unsure where to begin.

Grab a piece of paper or open your journal and without editing or filtering write down five things that you have always wanted to do or create; the things that light you up, even if they scare you. They don't have to be huge. Whatever your heart whispers, write it down.

Then circle one. Not the one you think you 'should' do but the one that you feel drawn to the most. Then ask yourself, *what is the smallest possible step I can take towards this?* It doesn't have to be perfect. You just need to begin. Maybe it's sending an email or doing some research or purchasing some art supplies. Take that first step, then the next. Every step forward brings clarity, giving passion and purpose the opportunity to build from these small, soul-aligned choices.

These three tools will help you to reconnect and check in with yourself. You don't have to wait until you have it all figured out and you certainly don't need a ten-year plan. Your purpose is not some big, unachievable moment in the far distance, it's how you show up in your everyday life. It's how you love, how you care, how you express who you are.

You are already purposeful by simply being here on Earth. You are already enough. And if you've forgotten that, I'm here to remind you.

If you take one thing from this chapter, let it be this:

You are here to be you. Fully and freely, with all your light and your lessons. You are here to grow, to soften, to stretch, to love and to help others feel more seen, more safe and more alive, simply because you existed.

Your purpose is not outside of you. It lives within you and it always has. You don't need to go searching, you just need to come home to yourself.

And if you need support along the way, someone to help you navigate the noise, to reconnect with your passion and to remember your why, I am here.

As a coach, my work is to help women like you come back to yourself. To quiet the noise, untangle the stories and reconnect with what lights you up from within. You don't have to do it alone.

If your heart is nudging you right now, trust it. That whisper is worth listening to.

ABOUT VIKKI

Vikki Speller is a heart-led women's coach, mindfulness and meditation teacher, international speaker, and bestselling author who has dedicated her life to empowering others through self-love, intuition, and connection. Since founding *Intuition Plus* in 2008, she has facilitated transformational one-on-one coaching, women's circles, retreats, speaking engagements, and creative offerings that inspire deep personal growth.

With a background in holistic counselling, energy healing, and intuitive guidance, Vikki supports individuals to overcome challenges, make aligned decisions, and live in harmony with your true selves. She creates nurturing spaces where women feel seen, supported, and safe to grow. Her approach blends practical tools with soulful insight, helping people reconnect with their inner wisdom, build emotional resilience, and lead more purposeful lives. Whether through private sessions or group experiences, Vikki gently guides women to honour their truth and embrace their worth.

A passionate advocate for emotional wellbeing from an early age, Vikki is the inspiring author of the beloved children's books *Finding the Magic of Love* and *The Magical Friendship Spell*. These beautifully illustrated stories promote mindfulness, self-love, and positive mindset practices, featuring affirmations and practical tools for children, parents, and educators. Her upcoming children's books and affirmation card packs continue this mission, encouraging confidence, kindness, and compassion in the next generation.

For adults, Vikki's *Mandalas of Reflection – Colouring and Journaling* is a soulful mindfulness resource that invites users to slow down, reflect, and reconnect with themselves through creative expression and guided journaling. Her work speaks to those seeking greater clarity, inner peace, and self-discovery with more powerful offerings currently underway.

Vikki's voice is also found in bestselling anthologies, docufilms, and podcasts. As a regular columnist for Holistic Bliss Magazine, Vikki shares insights drawn from lived experience and deep spiritual connection.

Based in Queensland, Australia, Vikki cherishes time with her family and lives in alignment with the values she teaches. Her work is a testament to the belief that we all hold the power to create lives filled with meaning, magic and self-love, and that it's never too early or too late to begin.

Website: www.vikkispeller.com/
Instagram: www.instagram.com/vikki_speller_intuition_plus/
Facebook: www.facebook.com/intuitionplus.vikkispeller
LinkedIn: www.linkedin.com/in/vikki-speller-author-coaching-intuition-plus
TikTok: @vikki_speller

www.ingramcontent.com/pod-product-compliance
Lightning Source LLC
Chambersburg PA
CBHW020529080526
44583CB00013B/796